Write to the Heart

Wit & Wisdom of Women Writers

Edited by
Amber Coverdale Sumrall

 The Crossing Press
Freedom, CA 95019

For the women in my writing group—
Lin, Ellen, Maude, Joan, Candida, Kathy, and Dena
—where never is heard a discouraging word.

Cover art & design and interior art & design
by AnneMarie Arnold

Printed in the U.S.A.

Library of Congress Cataloging-in-Publication Data

Write to the heart : quotes by women writers / edited by Amber Coverdale Sumrall.
        p. cm.
    ISBN 0-89594--566-5   ISBN 0-89594-550-9 (pbk.)
    1. Women--Quotations. 2. Women--Quotations, maxims, etc.
I. Sumrall, Amber Coverdale
PN6081.5.W74   1992
081' .082--dc20
                                   92-11268
                                      CIP

Contents

Fame & Fortune . . . 1

Wit & Wisdom . . . 8

Women . . . 17

Transformation . . . 24

Time . . . 32

Process . . . 39

Politics . . . 49

Childhood . . . 59

Books . . . 67

Audience . . . 73

Beginning . . . 81

Courage . . . 89

515

Commitment . . . 95

Craft . . . 101

Love . . . 109

Memory . . . 116

Domestic Life . . . 123

Education . . . 132

Men . . . 140

Muse . . . 147

Resistance . . . 153

Silence . . . 160

Spirituality . . . 167

Truth . . . 173

Writer's Life . . . 181

Aging . . . 189

If the doors of my heart ever close,
I am as good as dead.
                    —*Mary Oliver*

How to pull straight from the heart?
How to continue, how to start?
                    —*Lorraine Duisit*

Preface

Once, I collected trading cards, Little Lulu comic books and Nancy Drew mystery stories. Now, I collect books of poetry by women and quotes by women writers. I jot the quotes down in notebooks, journals, or on scraps of paper, which are sometimes found weeks later between the pages of books, or at the bottom of my backpack. I have been collecting them for years. They are the messages I would like to find in my fortune cookies. When my own poems and stories won't come, they soothe and inspire, encourage me to be patient. Words of passion and strength. Remedies for psychic distress. Words of anger, hope and struggle. Meditations. Words of humor, wisdom.

These quotes have been compiled from small press publications, books, reviews, memoirs, interviews, workshops, speeches. I did not record them with the idea of putting them into a book. When I realized there were almost a thousand I decided to categorize them, to create an anthology of quotes by women writers. I grew up almost exclusively with male authors, their language and viewpoints. Occasionally, I came across stories or poems by women, a few books. Although there are now many published women writers, they seldom have the focus or status of male writers— in academia, in the publishing industry, in book reviews. Rarely are they quoted. *Write To The Heart* is one way, for me, of restoring balance and perspective. To the speakers and writers of these words I give my heartfelt thanks.

—*Amber Coverdale Sumrall*

Fame & Fortune

Fame is a comic distinction shared with Roy Rogers' horse and Miss Watermelon of 1955.

—*Flannery O'Connor*

A lot of people are always into thinking they can become famous. You know if you're talking fame, you're not a serious person.

—*Nikki Giovanni*

When we were young we all wanted to be in the big important quarterlies, like the *Partisan Review* and *The Hudson Review.* Now you don't even send them your work. They're all ossified. They've gone on too long. They ought to creep into the ground and throw dirt on themselves.

—*Carolyn Kizer*

The best young writers are convinced they need blurbs from famous writers before an editor will even read the first page of a manuscript. If this is true, then the editorial system that prevails today stinks. And let's start reforming it.

—*Diane Wakoski*

Fame & Fortune

Fame means millions of people have a wrong idea of who you are.

—*Erica Jong*

I do want to get rich but I never want to do what there is to do to get rich.

—*Gertrude Stein*

I sense in a good many books, even in books by the best writers, an anxiety about how it will do in the marketplace. You can feel it on the page, a sort of sweat of calculation.

—*Elizabeth Hardwick*

I'm cautious about making money at something that is not the love of my life.

—*Emily Prager*

You get an advance and then you go out and get the facial and go to Jiffy Lube instead of getting someone to put some oil in your car. You do that for about three weeks and life goes back to normal and there is no money again for awhile.

—*Anne Lamont*

Fame & Fortune

The two most beautiful words in the English language are: "Check enclosed."

—*Dorothy Parker*

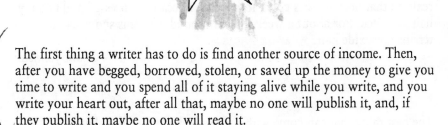

The first thing a writer has to do is find another source of income. Then, after you have begged, borrowed, stolen, or saved up the money to give you time to write and you spend all of it staying alive while you write, and you write your heart out, after all that, maybe no one will publish it, and, if they publish it, maybe no one will read it.

—*Ellen Gilchrist*

Being popular is important. Otherwise people might not like you.

—*Mimi Pond*

Success makes you ridiculous; you end up wearing nightgowns to dinner.

—*Natalie Goldberg*

Fame & Fortune

My expectations were never that I'd have a career that could bankroll anything more than typing paper.

—*Rosellen Brown*

After I published, I found life tremendously depressing. I guess I'm not like other people in that I had built such a fantasy life on what would happen when I became a real published writer. Of course, nothing happens. When I realized that nothing was going to happen, I became depressed and had my hair bleached. For about a week, I went around with this snow-white terrible peroxide hair.

—*Diane Johnson*

The best thing that can come with success is the knowledge that it is nothing to long for.
—*Liv Ullmann*

There's a difference between writing for a living and writing for life. If you write for a living you make enormous compromises, and you might not ever be able to uncompromise yourself. If you write for life you'll work hard; you'll do what's honest, not what pays.

—*Toni Morrison*

Fame & Fortune

My private measure of success is daily. If this were to be the last day of my life would I be content with it? To live in a harmonious balance of commitments and pleasures is what I strive for. Worldly success is an accident which may be catastrophic or lucky, depending on one's essential indifference to it.

—*Jane Rule*

I'd rather have roses on my table than diamonds on my neck.

—*Emma Goldman*

I wrote for twelve years and collected 250 rejection slips before getting any fiction published, so I guess outside reinforcement isn't all that important to me.

—*Lisa Alther*

Nothing stinks like a pile of unpublished writing, which remark I guess shows I still don't have a pure motive (O it's-such-fun-I-just-can't-stop-who-cares-if-it's-published-or-read) about writing.

—*Sylvia Plath*

Fame & Fortune

I've learned once again the lesson that I believe all but the most sucessful writers (and acclaim has other perils) have to keep relearning throughout the course of their careers: the world does not need one's work, and has endlessly varied ways of reminding one of the fact.

—Jan Clausen

To be any sort of competent writer, one must keep one's psychological distance from the supreme artists.

—Cynthia Ozick

Celebrated women writers are usually those who describe life at a distance from their personal selves.

—Jane Lazarre

If I wrote about heterosexual love and created admirable (that is, nice and important) men I bet my writing income would be tripled.

—Joanna Russ

With fiction you can have the dream of selling stuff, but with poetry — forget it. You cannot have even the illusion of making a living writing poetry.

—Tama Janowitz

Fame & Fortune

The choice between starving and being eaten is an exotic one.

—*Francine du Plessix Gray*

Nobody can tell me what to write because nobody owns me and nobody pulls my strings. I have not been writing to make money or earn my living. I have taught school as my vocation. Writing is my life, but it is an avocation nobody can buy.

—*Margaret Walker*

Writing is a democratic act. There is no hierarchy. So what if you are the recipient of the Nobel Prize in literature? You have to wake up the next day and start another story.

—*Natalie Goldberg*

You're only as good as your last book.

—*Nikki Giovanni*

I had published two volumes of poetry to critical acclaim, and received recognition and awards, but it was clear to me that poetry was not the language of the land.

—*Erica Jong*

Wit & Wisdom

Be happy. It's one way of being wise.

—*Colette*

Those who never complain are never pitied.

—*Jane Austen*

Writers, however mature and wise and eminent, are children at heart.

—*Edna O'Brien*

Maybe being oneself is always an acquired taste.

—*Patricia Hampl*

I frankly think that one of the things that make artists different from other people is that they are more intelligent.

—*Diane Wakoski*

I've always felt that a person's intelligence is directly reflected by the number of conflicting points of view he can entertain simultaneously on the same topic.

—*Lisa Alther*

Since when was genius respectable?

—*Elizabeth Barrett Browning*

I have often wished I had time to cultivate modesty. But I am too busy thinking about myself.

—*Edith Sitwell*

Worry less about what other people think about you, and more about what you think of them.

—*Fay Weldon*

You can't go around hoping that most people have sterling moral characters. The most you can hope for is that people will pretend that they do.

—*Fran Lebowitz*

It is very easy to forgive others their mistakes; it takes more grit and gumption to forgive them for having witnessed your own.

—*Jessamyn West*

Character builds slowly, but it can be torn down with incredible swiftness.

—*Faith Baldwin*

I believe talent is like electricity. We don't undertstand electricity. We use it. You can plug into it and light up a lamp, keep a heart pump going, light a cathedral, or you can electrocute a person with it. Electricity will do all that. It makes no judgement. I think talent is like that. I believe every person is born with talent.

—*Maya Angelou*

The act of longing for something will always be more intense than the requiting of it.

—*Gail Godwin*

All of writing is a huge lake. There are great rivers that feed the lake, like Tolstoy and Dostoyevsky. And there are mere trickles, like Jean Rhys. All that matters is feeding the lake. I don't matter. The lake matters.

— Jean Rhys

I love music but that doesn't mean I know anything about it. I think a good many poems fall in the category with songs; they are at least singable.

—Janet Lewis

I find that most people know what a story is until they sit down to write one.

—Flannery O'Connor

There ain't no answer. There ain't going to be any answer. There never has been an answer. That's the answer.

—Gertrude Stein

Truly nothing is to be expected but the unexpected.

—Alice James

Wit & Wisdom

Art must take reality by surprise.

—*Francoise Sagan*

Isn't poetry a form of prophecy, and aren't prophets known for their talent for flourishing in inhospitable deserts and other bleak surroundings?

—*Jan Clausen*

Sanity is the most profound moral option of our time.

—*Renata Adler*

I want much more material; I am tired of my little stories like birds bred in cages.

— *Katherine Mansfield*

There are only two or three human stories, and they go on repeating themselves as fiercely as if they had never happened before.

—*Willa Cather*

The universe is made of stories, not of atoms.

—Muriel Rukeyser

The meaning of the story is the story.

—Flannery O'Connor

Poetry is a dumb Buddha who thinks a donkey is as important as a diamond.

—Natalie Goldberg

Everybody gets so much information all day long that they lose their common sense.

—Gertrude Stein

Television is the great bane of the late twentieth century. It's made people moronic, its robbed people of their ability to think. It's done tremendous damage, and every single household that has a small child should take it and throw it out the window.

—Laurie Colwin

Wit & Wisdom

I have come to the conclusion, after many years of sometimes sad experience, that you cannot come to any conclusion at all.

—*Vita Sackville-West*

Expecting life to treat you well because you are a good person is like expecting an angry bull not to charge because you are a vegetarian.

—*Shari R. Barr*

Contradiction is the criterion of reality.

—*Simone Weil*

Change is an easy panacea. It takes character to stay in one place and be happy there.

—*Elizabeth Clarke Dunn*

No mockery in the world ever sounds to me as hollow as that of being told to *cultivate* happiness . . . Happiness is not a potato, to be planted in mold, and tilled with manure.

—*Charlotte Bronte*

Wit & Wisdom

Poems aren't postcards to send home.

—Anne Sexton

After the first twenty times somebody tells you that they were reincarnated Indians, you have to have a humorous perspective or you are going to put somebody up against the wall.

—Linda Hogan

The cure for anything is salt water — sweat, tears, or the sea.

—Isak Dinesen

My "I" is a flash of chemicals.

—Cynthia Ozick

I'm less interested in poems as neat little compacts of snapped mirror, with myself inside.

—Heather McHugh

Wit & Wisdom

If writing comes before people then it loses all value. Writing is only words on paper.

—*Fay Weldon*

The opposite of talking isn't listening. The opposite of talking is waiting.
—*Fran Lebowitz*

I do not want people to be very agreeable, as it saves me the trouble of liking them a great deal.

—*Jane Austen*

Life is either always a tight-rope or a feather bed. Give me the tight-rope.
—*Edith Wharton*

Everything that isn't writing is fun.

—*Dorothy Parker*

Women

If you're a woman writer, sometime, somewhere, you will be asked: *Do you think of yourself as a writer first, or as a woman first?* Look Out. Whoever asks this hates and fears both writing and women.

—*Margaret Atwood*

Any woman born with a great gift in the sixteenth century would certainly have gone crazed, shot herself or ended her days in some lonely cottage outside the village, half witch, half wizard, feared and mocked at.

—*Virginia Woolf*

Women who wrote novels were quite often perceived as invalids.

—*Joan Didion*

The story behind the injustices endured by women writers is the story of womankind. At one time we were considered contaminated; we were later elevated to merely brainless.

—*Diana Gleasner*

We aren't here to make pretty things.

—*Monique Wittig*

Women

My work has been heard into existence by other women.
—Susan Griffin

Hetero-relations deprive women of a certain type of language
characterized by an integrity of reactions, a simplicity of gestures,
and an unaffected expression of feeling for each other.
—Janice G. Raymond

If I had to characterize one quality as the genius of feminist
thought, culture, and action, it would be the *connectivity*.
—Robin Morgan

It's a rare occasion when I read women's work and can find nothing
that belongs to me. Whether they speak to love, the mountains of
Kenya, or the cooking pot, women poets call out to me as no male
poet of equal skill and emotion ever has.
—Terri L. Jewell

I've never doubted that everything I wrote was in a woman's voice,
including "and" and "the."
—Jan Clausen

Women

Women tend to qualify more than men. They put "perhaps" and "I think" and use diminutives more than men.

—*Gail Godwin*

Women have been called queens for a long time, but the kingdom given them isn't worth ruling.

—*Louisa May Alcott*

It is hardly surprising that women concentrate on the way they look instead of what is in their minds since not much has been put in their minds to begin with.

—*Mary Wollstonecraft Shelley*

The gender gap is still there but no longer yawns as an all but unleapable chasm. Women poets need no longer hide behind first initials. Editors of national magazines no longer reply that they loved your poem, but they published a woman last month . . .

—*Maxine Kumin*

Women

I'm a feminist, and God knows I'm loyal to my sex, and you must remember that from my very early days, when this city was scarcely safe from buffaloes, I was in the struggle for equal rights for women. But when we paraded through the catcalls of men and when we chained ourselves to lamp-posts to try to get our equality — we didn't foresee *those* female writers.

—Dorothy Parker

I am not the darling of the feminists. They think I am too preoccupied with old-fashioned themes like love and longing. Though one woman in Ms. magazine pointed out that I send bulletins from battle fronts where other women do not go.

—Edna O'Brien

Show me a woman who doesn't feel guilty and I'll show you a man.

—Erica Jong

Where I can get irritable is when you have your Jeanne Kirkpatrick sensibility calling itself feminist.

—Robin Morgan

Women

I think that the women who can get beyond the feeling of having to correct history will save a lot of time. The women who are trying to correct man's nature are wasting their time . . . in men's heads everything's still the same . . . I don't care about men. I've given up on them, personally.

—Marguerite Duras

My true friends have always given me that supreme proof of devotion, a spontaneous aversion for the man I loved.

—Colette

The major concrete achievement of the women's movement in the 1970's was the Dutch treat.

—Nora Ephron

Girls who put out are tramps. Girls who don't are ladies. This is, however, a rather archaic usage of the word. Should one of you boys happen upon a girl who doesn't put out, do not jump to the conclusion that you have found a lady. What you have probably found is a lesbian.

—Fran Lebowitz

Women

The only thing that matched the wildness I felt inside when I wrote was kissing a woman.

—*Natalie Goldberg*

Some of us are becoming the men we wanted to marry.

—*Gloria Steinem*

Without the periods of passion there would be no content for feminist art. Without the period of lonely wandering there would be no artist, for she would long ago have drowned in one ocean or another.

—*Jane Lazarre*

All women's boundaries are crossed at one time or another and they are crossed continually.

—*Elizabeth Winthrop*

I've been called a Meduse, an Octopus, etc. The attack being: here is a woman who doesn't use words in a soft, compliant way; therefore, she is an evil witch.

—*Margaret Atwood*

Women

In my fiction and that of many women, the focus starts close-up, then the world pans out. When men are close-in, their observations are cerebral, almost opinions — in men, the mind is connected to the brain. In women, the mind is connected to the heart, which influences the way they think.

—Amy Tan

A lot of us were the higher power for our families, mostly the girls. We took on fixing people and we took on using our blood as crazy glue and would lose blood to fix other people and became givers, just huge givers. And part of it was about having very low self-esteem. It wasn't all about this radiant large heart that God had given us.

—Anne Lamont

One is not born a woman, one becomes one.

—Simone de Beauvoir

At certain times I have no race. I am *me*. I belong to no race or time. I am the eternal feminine with its string of beads.

—Zora Neale Hurston

Transformation

Creativity is really the structuring of magic.

—Anne Kent Rush

Once we recognize what it is we are feeling, once we recognize we can feel deeply, love deeply, can feel joy, the we will demand that all parts of our lives produce that kind of joy.

—Audre Lorde

In the most modern cities, a person who works with a computer may very well ask a spiritualist to read his future in the cards or to sell him a love potion, because he sees that everyday reality seems to be slipping from him, that he is surrounded by shadows.

—Isabel Allende

Art is the method of levitation, in order to separate one's self from enslavement by the earth.

—Anais Nin

Transformation

Women have always been the interior decorators, rather than the
architects. I would like to propose that the image which used to be
decoration in poetry is now becoming the building, the room iself.

—Diane Wakoski

A poem consists of a number of words which, taken together, create
a single new word, the only possible word to name completely that
thought which the poem is.

—Jane Hirshfield

To define oneself as authentically as possible from within has
become the major female enterprise in poetry. Not what our fathers
and mothers told us, not what our teachers expected, not what our
lovers suppose, not necessarily what literature and mythology,
however beautiful and compelling, tells us.

—Alicia Ostriker

Poetry has its own laws speaking for the life of the planet. It is a
language that wants to bring back together what the other words
have torn apart.

—Linda Hogan

Often a poem is where an emotional or metaphysical truce takes place.

—*Diane Ackerman*

The necessity of poetry has to be stated over and over to those who have reason to fear its power or to those who still believe that language is "only words" and that an old language is good enough for our description of the world we are trying to transform.

—*Adrienne Rich*

It takes awhile for our experience to sift through our consciousness.

—*Natalie Goldberg*

The transforming of the contemporary scene is what I now ask of all American writers. I urge them to be the individual interpreters of this deep concern which can never find a place upon the air until a purer wavelength has been found for it.

—*Kay Boyle*

Transformation

I think that Native American literature is useful to anybody who's trying to move from one world to another.

—*Paula Gunn Allen*

Someone said you hear words, but I always see things when I hear words.

—*Amy Tan*

I've dreamt in my life dreams that have stayed with me ever after, and changed my ideas; they've gone through and through me, like wine through water, and altered the color of my mind.

—*Emily Bronte*

I know I walk in and out of several worlds every day.

—*Joy Harjo*

Transformation

A lot of times messages are coming through to us and we receive them with fear because we've been trained to be fearful and that fear is the thing that ruins the charm. My plant dying would be for me the sign that I've come to a point of stagnation. I've got to go back to the root of the problem. I've got to take the plant out of its pot, look at it, see what is not being done. I've got to lay that book down and read what is missing.

—*Luisah Teish*

Just because everything is different doesn't mean anything has changed.

—*Irene Poter*

I would really feel badly if somebody said, "Well, I read you in '69 and I'm glad to say, you haven't changed." That would *ruin* my day. That would send me into a glass of something and I don't drink.

—*Nikki Giovanni*

I am not interested in man-woman things much. In-out. Or love. I am interested in loneliness, obsession, desperation. . . . Transformation is what I'm interested in the most.

—*Joy Williams*

Transformation

My literary agenda begins by acknowledging that America has transformed *me*. It does not end until I show how I (and the hundreds of thousands like me) have transformed America.

—*Bharati Mukherjee*

You will not grow if you sit in a beautiful flower garden, but you will grow if you are sick, if you are in pain, if you experience losses, and if you do not put your head in the sand, but take the pain and learn to accept it, not as a curse or punishment but as a gift to you with a very, very specific purpose.

—*Elizabeth Kubler-Ross*

Pain is important: how we evade it, how we succumb to it, how we deal with it, how we transcend it.

—*Audre Lorde*

I will write myself into well-being.

—*Nancy Mairs*

Transformation

The growing automatization and joylessness of twentieth-century work may lead us to covet more than ever artists' freedom to make the illicit licit, to transform through the alchemy of imagination the actuality of boredom and of death.

—Francine du Plessix Gray

Because poems, as in no other way we use language, are able to carry the destiny of such a complex synthesis, they are the best and oldest forms we have for attending and absolving grief, for bringing it into a useful relationship to those things we are about to do toward a future.

—Tess Gallagher

Language for me is action. To speak words that have been unspoken, to imagine that which is unimaginable, is to create the place in which change (action) occurs. I do believe our acts are limited — ultimately — only by what we fail or succeed in conceptualizing.

—Judith McDaniel

I'm not sure a bad person can write a good book. If art doesn't make us better, then what on earth is it for?

—Alice Walker

Transformation

A book of poems chronicles the poet's many selves, and as such knows more about the poet than the poet does at any given time, including the time when the book is finished and yet another self holds her book of previous selves in her hand.

—Diane Ackerman

For women, then, poetry is not a luxury. It is a vital necessity of our existence. It forms the quality of the light within which we predicate our hopes and dreams toward survival and change, first made into language, then into idea, then into more tangible action. Poetry is the way we help give name to the nameless so it can be thought.

—Audre Lorde

Time

Women tell time by the body. They are like clocks. They are always fastened to the earth, listening for its small animal noises.

—Anne Sexton

All time is during. That is why it is so hard to exist in the present. Already we are speeding ahead so fast that we can only look back to see where we have been.

—Tess Gallagher

This has been a most wonderful evening. Gertrude has said things tonight it'll take her ten years to understand.

—Alice B. Toklas

What person in the world goes through life in a straight line? I think that most people, whether aware of it or not, are never in one place or one time. We have this idea of a linear time imposed on us. That's why we have such trouble with concepts like eternity, heaven and hell. If you start looking at it, it's all here and now.

—Gail Godwin

No matter how long I live there will never be a dull moment.

—Harriet Doerr

Time

Short stories are a piece of time. The novel is a way of life.

—*Toni Cade Bambara*

A novel is really like a symphony . . . where instrument after instrument has to come in at its own time, and no other.

—*Katherine Anne Porter*

Once a poem begins, I can make a total commitment. It doesn't matter if it takes a day, a week, or six weeks. I can stay with it because I have faith in that original impulse.

—*Maxine Kumin*

We say we waste time, but that is impossible. We waste ourselves.

—*Alice Bloch*

Leave the dishes unwashed and the demands on your time unanswered. Be ruthless and refuse to do what people ask of you.

—*Lynne Sharon Schwartz*

Time

You cannot just waste time. Otherwise you'll die to regret it.

—*Harriet Doerr*

I worked at it for years and years but I was never a great poet.

—*Grace Paley*

Writing is static. The story will remain as printed for the next two hundred years and it's not going to change. That really bothers me, because what would be wonderful would be for the words to change on the page every time, but they can't. The way I tried to solve this problem was to keep ambiguity in the writing all the time.

—*Maxine Hong Kingston*

The poem is much more involved in the moment. It can be a moment which intersects with many other past moments and future moments, but it really finally has to happen in a shorter time than the story.

—*Tess Gallagher*

The moment of change is the only poem.

—*Adrienne Rich*

Time

We write to taste life twice, in the moment, and in retrospection.

—Anais Nin

The events in our lives happen in a sequence in time, but in their significance to ourselves they find their own order — perhaps not possibly — chronological.

—Eudora Welty

If I don't have my two-hour fix in the morning I just don't feel right.

—Gail Godwin

The best time for me to write is when other people are asleep. I am not needed in their dreams.

—Elizabeth Jolley

A perfect day to write is to write two hours, work in the yard two hours, and write ten pieces of mail, that's all I want to do. It never works out that way — or not often.

—Carolyn See

Time

I believe there are more urgent and honorable occupations than the incomparable waste of time we call suffering.

—Colette

How slowly one comes to understand anything!

—May Sarton

As time passes we all get better at blazing a trail through the thicket of advice.

—Margot Bennett

When we speak of a poem "working," we mean the muscle, activity, the liveliness of a poem. Whether a poem is working in real time or imaginary time, stopped time or simultaneous time, the language must literally and figuratively be "moving."

—Jane Miller

Time is a dressmaker specializing in alterations.

—Faith Baldwin

Time

The poem reminds us that the past is not only that which happened but also that which could have happened but did not.

—*Tess Gallagher*

I never work at night because by then the shackles of the day are around me.

—*Edna O'Brien*

I work from midnight to around three every morning on my writing. At that time the house is quiet.

—*Sonia Sanchez*

I learned how to work by having held jobs since I was fourteen, and not really working very hard at them. Through all these jobs, writing was the thing I saved for — I waited for that sacred, peaceful time late at night when I could go on and on. And now that I can write almost full-time, I unplug the phone and close the door and just stick with it. I don't ever go out for lunch and I don't take vacations. I like to be awake when no one else is: either just before dawn in the morning or late, late at night. Silence helps.

—*Mona Simpson*

Time

When does writing have an end? What is the warning sign? A trembling of the hand?

—*Colette*

There are years that ask questions and years that answer.

—*Zora Neale Hurston*

It is never too late to be what you might have been.

—*George Eliot*

Process

Look for a long time at what pleases you, and longer still at what pains you.

—*Colette*

I'm not sure I understand the process of writing. There is, I'm sure, something strange about imaginative concentration. The brain slowly begins to function in a different way, to make mysterious connections.

—*Elizabeth Hardwick*

When I'm writing I don't dream much; its like the dreaming gets used in the writing.

—*Ursula K. Le Guin*

What writing practice, like Zen practice, does is to bring you back to the natural state of mind, the wilderness of your mind where there are no refined rows of gladiolas.

—*Natalie Goldberg*

Nothing you write, if you hope to be good, will ever come out as you first hoped.

—*Lillian Hellman*

Process

If I had to give one word which serves my poetry more than any other, it might be "uncertainty." Uncertainty which leads to exploration, to the articulation of fears, to the loss of the kind of confidence that provides answers too quickly, too superficially.

—*Tess Gallagher*

I write about things I don't have any resolutions for, and when I'm finished, I think I know a little bit more about it. I don't write out of what I know. It's what I don't know that stimulates me. I merely know enough to get started.

—*Toni Morrison*

The preoccupation of the novelist: how to capture the living moments, was answered by the diary. You write while they are alive. You do not preserve them in alcohol until the moment you are ready to write about them.

—*Anais Nin*

I carry my journal with me almost all the time. If I have poems that just come, I write them in there as if they were journal entries. I try to keep my journal on a day to day basis.

—*Ntozake Shange*

Process

The writer should never be ashamed of staring. There is nothing that does not require his attention.

—*Flannery O'Connor*

I once wrote that the best way to write was to do so as if one were already dead: afraid of no one's reactions, answerable to no one for one's views. I still think that is the way to write.

—*Nadine Gordimer*

Process

I have yet to know the use of a poem the way I know the use of a hammer. Yet I feel a poem is surely a tool.

—Karen Brodine

There is a definite spin-off from one poem to another, because in the process of narrowing in on a subject a lot of peripheral ideas occur which then struggle to announce themselves.

—Maxine Kumin

I think of writing anything at all as a kind of high-wire act. The minute you start putting words on paper you're eliminating possibilites.

—Joan Didion

One must avoid ambition in order to write. Otherwise something else is the goal: some kind of power beyond the power of language. And the power of language, it seems to me, is the only kind of power a writer is entitled to.

—Cynthia Ozick

Some poems are never finished.

— Jayne Cortez

Process

I'm in favor of people keeping their writing to themselves for years. Musicians know its dumb to go public when they can't keep the chord changes right.

—*Bobbie Louise Hawkins*

It is fatal to one's artistic life to talk about something that is in process.

—*Denise Levertov*

For years I thought the only "proper" way to write was to start a poem and plug away at it until it was done — sort of like finishing all the food on your plate at dinner.

—*Rita Dove*

After thirteen years I at last finished a novel. The first seven years were spent in a kind of apprenticeship - the book that came out of that time was abandoned without much regret. A second one was finished in six weeks and buried. It took six years to write the third novel, and this one was finally published.

—*Cynthia Ozick*

Process

The passage is through, not over, not by, not around but through.
—Cherrie Moraga

It's easy to lose the energy you need for a long piece unless the characters are surprising you and showing you something new every week or even every month or every other paragraph.
—Alice McDermott

It's gotten to the point where it's impossible for me to create new characters because the old ones keep grabbing up all the roles.
—Ellen Gilchrist

I like to think of what happens to characters in good novels and stories as knots - things keep knotting up. And by the end of the story — readers see an "unknotting" of sorts. Not what they expect, not the easy answers you get on TV, not wash and wear philosophies, but a reproduction of believable emotional experiences.
—Terry McMillan

Process

Everyone has their drug, whether it's liquor or dope or coffee. Mine is a certain kind of Swiss coffee that takes a half hour to brew. But I would try anything once for work. Anything.

—Mona Simpson

The solitude of writing is also quite frightening. It's quite close sometimes to madness, one just disappears for a day and loses touch.

—Nadine Gordimer

I believe poets have to be inside their poems somewhere, or the poem won't work.

—Joy Harjo

I think that one's art is a growth inside one. I do not think one can explain growth. It is silent and subtle. One does not keep digging up a plant to see how it grows.

—Emily Carr

It is as if my whole body were flowing out in words like blood and only a husk is left for everything else.

—Michele Murray

Process

I feel very much that the person I am was there, as I am now, at six or seven and all this stuff was layered on to me — defenses and veils and screens, which I use a lot, and to get back to myself I simply had to peel. So much of our growing up is breaking out, freeing ourselves, and for different people that comes at different times. For me it was in my forties.

—*Lynne Sharon Schwartz*

If you don't keep and mature your force and above all have time and quiet to perfect your work, you will be writing things not much better than you did five years ago.

—*Tillie Olson*

I think that some of the worst poems in the English language are written by poets about how they make a poem.

—*Maxine Kumin*

I'm not interested in reading or writing what I already think. The whole point of writing as I do is to go forward as a thinker or philosopher.

—*Lyn Hejinian*

Process

I'm essentially undisciplined. I do a lot of thinking, a lot of reading, but I wouldn't recommend my writing method. I write when it's compelling.

—*Nikki Giovanni*

I write my poems on scraps of paper because I want to carry them in my address book. I'm likely to read them at a moment's notice.

—*Gwendolyn Brooks*

Breathe in experience. Breathe out poetry.

—*Muriel Rukeyser*

There is a gap between the journal and my poetry. I write this stuff in my journal, and sometimes I cannot even read my journals because there is so much pain and rage in them. I'll put it away in a drawer, and six months, a year or so later, I'll pick up the journal, and there will be the seeds of poems.

—*Audre Lorde*

Writing is making sense of life. You work your whole life and perhaps you've made sense of one small area.

—*Nadine Gordimer*

Process

If you are writing anything that matters, your body tells you where to stop. Writing a poem is physical.

—*Kate Braverman*

I haven't a clue as to how my story will end. But that's all right. When you set out on a journey and night covers the road, you don't conclude that the road has vanished. And how else could we discover the stars?

—*Nancy Willard*

It is good to have an end to journey towards; but it is the journey that matters, in the end.

—*Ursula K. LeGuin*

Politics

Survival is a form of resistance.

—*Meridel Le Sueur*

I do not weep at the world — I am too busy sharpening my oyster knife.

—*Zora Neale Hurston*

Whenever I write out of anger or terror, there is a sense in which the terror or anger — at specific injustice, mass opression, torture, or simply unwilled solitude — is a cry against our race toward a common suicide.

—*Jane Cooper*

Politics

Oppression involves a failure of the imagination: the failure to imagine the full humanity of other human beings.

—*Margaret Atwood*

The English language contains almost as many derogatory words for blacks as for women and it is a constantly undermining task to structure one's world with a language that daily and deliberately denies one's humanity, and to use language in a manner that the dominant white group deems appropriate.

—*Dale Spender*

We need to raise our voices a little more, even as they say to us "This is so uncharacteristic of you." Invisibility is not a natural state for anyone.

—*Mitsuye Yamada*

And where were the Black poets? And who were the women poets I might reasonably emulate? And wasn't there, ever, a great poet who was crazy about Brooklyn or furious about war?

—*June Jordan*

Politics

Poetry isn't revolution but a way of knowing why it must come.
—*Adrienne Rich*

I probably have not killed anyone in America because I write, I've maintained good controls over myself by writing.
—*Sonia Sanchez*

If it takes head-on collisions, let's do it: this polite timidity is killing us.
—*Cherrie Moraga*

It is not so much a question of whether the lion will one day lie down with the lamb, but whether human beings will ever be able to lie down with any other creature or being at all.
—*Alice Walker*

As long as the family and the myth of family have not been destroyed, women will still be oppressed.
—*Simone de Beauvoir*

Politics

The history of men's opposition to women's emancipation is more interesting perhaps than the story of that emancipation itself.

—*Virginia Woolfe*

Protest is an inherent part of my work. You can't just not write about protest themes or not sing about them. It's a part of life. If I don't agree with a part of life, then my work has to address it.

—*Maya Angelou*

If I had to name one quality as the genius of patriarchy, it would be compartmentalization, the capacity for institutionalizing disconnection. Intellect severed from emotion. Thought separated from action. Science split from art. The earth itself divided; national borders. Human beings categorized: by sex, age, race, ethnicity, sexual preference, height, weight, class, religion, physical ability, ad nauseum. The personal isolated from the political. Sex divorced from love. The material ruptured from the spiritual. Law detached from justice. Vision disassociated from reality.

—*Robin Morgan*

Politics

I have a profound belief that anything (well, almost anything) a woman writes is of use to women. That is our only "political obligation."
                                        —*Rosellen Brown*

It's faintly obscene for most American writers to bemoan their difficulties when writers in other parts of the world are having trouble even staying alive or out of prison.
                                        —*Lisa Alther*

Racism forces white humanity to underestimate the intelligence, emotion, and creativity of black humanity.
                                        —*Margaret Walker*

No art can develop until it penetrates deeply into the life of the people.
                                        —*Meridel Le Sueur*

I cannot and will not cut my conscience to fit this year's fashions.
                                        —*Lillian Hellman*

Politics

There is no such thing as nonpolitical poetry. The time, however, to determine what those politics will be is not the moment of taking pen to paper, but during the whole of one's life. We are responsible for the quality of our vision, we have a say in the shaping of our sensibility. In the many thousand daily choices we make, we create ourselves and the voice with which we speak and work.

—Carolyn Forche

Re-vision — the act of looking back, of seeing with fresh eyes, of entering an old text from a new critical direction — is for women more than a chapter in cultural history: it is an act of survival. Until we can understand the assumptions in which we are drenched we cannot know ourselves. And this drive to self-knowledge, for women, is more than a search for identity: it is part of our refusal of the self-destructiveness of male-dominated society.

—Adrienne Rich

Real solemn history I cannot be interested in . . . The quarrels of popes and kings, with wars or pestilences on every page; the men all so good for nothing, and hardly any women at all.

—Jane Austen

Politics

I don't know of an uglier word I've ever been called in my life than "bulldyke." I was so haunted by this for many years that I finally decided to take the word by the horns and find out why this strange word is in the vernacular. I've traced it to a Celtic queen who fought against the Romans in A.D. 61 during the reign of Nero and nearly won. Her name was Boadicea.

—Judy Grahn

How could I possibly overthrow the government when I can't even keep my dog down.

—Dorothy Parker

One of my correspondents has me convinced that the human race would be saved if the world became one huge nudist colony. I keep thinking how much harder it would be to carry concealed weapons.

—Cyra McFadden

The most lethal weapon in the world's arsenal is not the neutron bomb or chemical warfare but the human mind that devises such things and puts them to use.

—Margaret Atwood

Politics

There is no metaphor for the end of the world and it is horrible to search for one.

—*Carolyn Forche*

What *is* it possible to know? I mean, beyond the fact that there are or are not wilted vegetables, and that the women do or do not have nice clothes. This is the question that haunts modern times: did you know? Did you know about Auschwitz? Did you know about My Lai? Did you know about the CIA in Chile? Did we know? When did we find out?

—*Patricia Hampl*

If I were anything from outer space, I would make a point to come into a black community because that's the only place where I would *at least* be given a chance. The first response of black people would not be to shoot me, stamp me out, poison me or somehow get rid of me. They would be curious about me. They would not do what your average cracker would do which is to wipe me out.

—*Nikki Giovanni*

Politics

I believe in subversion rather than straight-out confrontation.
—*Leslie Marmon Silko*

Sometimes, I feel discriminated against, but it does not make me angry. It merely astonishes me. How *can* anyone deny themselves the pleasure of my company? It's beyond me.
—*Zora Neale Hurston*

I sometimes have the sense that I live my life as a writer with my nose pressed against the wide, shiny plate glass window of the mainstream culture.
—*Jan Clausen*

Every writer is a cell on the body politic of America.
—*Sharon Olds*

Politics

And then it just seems preposterous. There I am, choosing my words so carefully, trying to build this pure, unanalyzable, transparent, honest thing in this dim room with the shades drawn and out there is the world, indecent, cruel, apathetic, a world where the seas are being trashed, the desert bladed, the wolves shot, the eagles poisoned, where people show up at planning and zoning meetings waving signs that say *My Family Can't Eat the Environment.* That sentence is ill, it is a virus of a sentence, and as a writer, I should be able to defeat it and its defenders handily. With the perfect words I should be able to point out, reasonably, that in fact the individual's family is eating the environment, that they are consuming it with sprawl and greed and materialistic hungers and turning it into — shit. But perfect words fail me. I don't want my words. I want to throttle this person, beat him over the head with his stupid sign.

— *Joy Williams*

Childhood

One hears one's childhood and it is ancient.

—*Kathleen Fraser*

Childhood

I grew up nestled in an enormous cradle, that powerful vessel which projects its rhythm on lyrical infinity.

—Colette

Children, like animals, use all their senses to discover the world.

—Eudora Welty

I learned that you should feel when writing, not like Lord Byron on a mountain top, but like a child stringing beads in kindergarten — happy, absorbed and quietly putting one bead on after another.

—Brenda Ueland

My words now must be as slow, as new, as single, as tentative as the steps I took going down the path away from the house, between the dark-branching tall dancers motionless against the winter shining.

—Ursula K. Le Guin

The poet between poems is like a child called into the house to peel potatoes for supper.

—Tess Gallagher

Childhood

When I was a child in Ireland, a spring would suddenly appear and yield forth buckets of beautiful clear water, then just as suddenly it would dry up. The water-diviners would come with their rods and sometimes another spring would be found. One has to be one's own water-diviner.

—*Edna O'Brien*

I had to grow up and learn to listen for the unspoken as well as the spoken.

—*Eudora Welty*

I write out of my own needs as a child.

—*Judy Blume*

I longed, when I was young, to write as well as Mark Twain. He was a man of very great shrewdness.

—*Rebecca West*

I wrote from the time I was four. It was my way of screaming and yelling, the primal scream. I wrote like a junkie, I had to have my daily fix.

—*M.F.K. Fisher*

Childhood

We never graduate from first grade. Over and over, we have to go back to the beginning.

—*Natalie Goldberg*

My first notebook was a Big Five tablet, given to me by my mother with the sensible suggestion that I stop whining and learn to amuse myself by writing down my thoughts. She returned the tablet to me a few years ago; the first entry is an account of a woman who believed herself to be freezing to death in the Artic night, only to find, when day broke, that she had stumbled onto the Sahara Desert, where she would die of the heat before lunch.

—*Joan Didion*

I fell into writing, I suppose, being one of those awful children who wrote verses.

—*Dorothy Parker*

I always thought I would be a writer, but I never really thought I had to do anything about it. I just thought it would happen to me the way getting married and having babies seemed to happen to everyone.

—*Lynne Sharon Schwartz*

Childhood

Because of my mother it never occured to me that you couldn't do what you wanted to do.

—Francine Prose

My mother would go out in a rowboat with a bunch of books and she would drop anchor and read to us. She would often read what she wanted to read and I suppose it was a way of getting her reading time in. But I think she genuinely enjoyed spending this time with us and I realized later just how amazing it was.

—Nancy Willard

I was the kind of child who always poked around wherever there was fear: to see what kind of a creature fear was.

—Luisa Valenzuela

In a Chinese family the mother pulls very tightly on the bond to a point where the daughter asks, "Why can't I know about such and such?" and the mother answers, "Because I haven't put it into your mind yet."

—Amy Tan

Childhood

I didn't want to be a boy, ever, but I was outraged that his height and intelligence were graces for him and gaucheries for me.

—Jane Rule

I was a very difficult child. I was a rebel from the time I can remember and I can remember fairly far back.

—Audre Lorde

I was a class clown, but everything always hurt. My feelings always hurt, my insides always hurt . . . . It's that thing about comparing your insides to other people's outsides. Other people's outsides look good, they look like a TV sitcom family.

—Anne Lamont

I think my father, and the rest of them invented the happy family and put it into movies to drive everyone crazy.

—Jill Robinson

Childhood

The truth about our childhood is stored up in our body, and although we can repress it, we can never alter it. Our intellect can be deceived, our feelings manipulated, our perceptions confused, and our body tricked with medication. But someday the body will present its bill, for it is as incorruptible as a child who, still whole in spirit, will accept no compromises or excuses, and it will not stop tormenting us until we stop evading the truth.

— Alice Miller

Creative minds have always been known to survive any kind of bad training.

—Anna Freud

The poet is one who is able to keep the fresh vision of the child alive.

—Anais Nin

I remember my father forbidding us to read *National Geographic* — not because there were photographs of naked women, but because the only naked women were dark-skinned; evidently Third World nudity did not offend Western sensibilities.

—Rita Dove

Childhood

I was told that if you liked doing something, it wasn't worth pursuing.

—*Amy Tan*

Getting away from being a "good girl" is important because it's impossible to be a "good girl" and a writer at the same time.

—*Lynne Sharon Schwartz*

Going home for most people is like trying to recapture childhood. It's an impossible task; you're not a child, and unless your parents have, by some grace of God, grown up with you, it's almost impossible to go back and stay and live.

—*Louise Erdrich*

Books

I read at a very young age, and I just read and read and read. That, more than any other influence or person, is what made me a writer.

—*Lynne Sharon Schwartz*

Reading is a private, intimate act for which we are accountable to no one.

—*Shirley Hazzard*

I hated childhood and spent it sitting behind a book waiting for adulthood to arrive.

—*Anne Tyler*

The greatest gift is the passion for reading. It is cheap, it consoles, it distracts, it excites, it gives you knowledge of the world and experience of a wide kind. It is a moral illumination.

—*Elizabeth Hardwick*

The one thing I regret is that I will never have time to read all the books I want to read.

—*Francoise Sagan*

Books

When you start reading in a certain way that's already the beginning of your writing. You're learning what you admire and you're learning to love other writers. The love of other writers is an important first step.

—Tess Gallagher

All the old houses that I knew when I was a child were full of books, bought generation after generation by members of the family. Nobody told you to read this or not to read that.

—Katherine Anne Porter

If I read a book that impresses me, I have to take myself firmly in hand before I mix with other people; otherwise they would think my mind rather queer.

—Anne Frank

Most women characters, in the books that I was reading when I was growing up, were passive. I remember that as a child, I used to identify in fairy tales with the prince because I could never fantasize about being in a castle — waiting.

—Irini Spanidou

When one of my male students writes a book with spiritual audacity, it's called an "epic urban tale" whereas the same book written by a woman is another neurotic housewife having a long identity crisis.

—*Kate Braverman*

I couldn't imagine writing a "woman's" book. What would it be, except maybe a cookbook?

—*Nancy Mairs*

In a book by a woman, rape won't be fun and women won't be simple-minded.

—*Marge Piercy*

Some say life is the thing, but I prefer reading.

—*Ruth Rendell*

Books

As far as the question of whether the writer can change the world . . . this much we know: that throughout history, so great has been the fear of the power of the writer, that books have been burned in the belief that putting the flame to the printed word also destroyed the conviction that lived in the word.

—*Kay Boyle*

The novel doesn't belong to Anglo people that much anymore.

—*Kate Braverman*

Modern novels are boring on the whole. Somebody told me I ought to read a wonderful thing about how a family of children buried Mum in a cellar under concrete and she began to smell. But that's the sole point of the story. Mum just smells. That's all that happens. It is not enough.

—*Rebecca West*

Having been unpopular in high school is not just cause for book publication.

—*Fran Lebowitz*

Books

The things that I like to read are very often the journals and letters, full of despair, of other writers. There's something very comforting in that — also something very voyeuristic.

—*Maxine Kumin*

If you like a book, maybe you'd better not meet the writer because she's only what's left over; most of her has gone into the book.

—*Jessamyn West*

I'm not very fond of poetry readings. I'd much rather read the book. I know I'm wrong. I've only been to a few poetry readings I could *bear.*

—*Elizabeth Bishop*

I'm reluctant to lose myself in another person's fictional world when I'm in the process of imagining one myself.

—*Ellen Schwamm*

What a sense of superiority it gives one to escape reading some book which everyone else is reading.

—*Alice James*

Books

I am addicted to novels but I've gotten increasingly finicky about what kind of prose I'm willing to stuff my mind with. Plot and narrative matter far less to me than they once did; what I want from a novel is a lesson in how to see and describe the world more precisely, with an almost scientific respect for nuance.

—Barbara Ehrenreich

To write and not read the best that has been written (and only the best; there's not time for anything less) is foolish. It's like a gardener putting in seeds where there is no ground.

—Gretel Ehrlich

I hardly ever go into a bookstore because, instead of buying, I would like to give away about five thousand of my seven thousand books, which are weighing on me like some suffocating plague.

—Elizabeth Hardwick

I read constantly. If I don't have a good book, I'm beside myself.

—Gail Godwin

Audience

The idea is to write it so that people hear it and it slides through the brain and goes straight to the heart.

—*Maya Angelou*

Readers, after all, are making the world with you. You give them the materials, but it's the readers who build that world in their own minds.

—*Ursula K. LeGuin*

You write in the fear that you won't interest anyone, that this is some peculiar neurosis of yours, some obsession. You just have to give it and hope that people can understand you. It's something of a miracle when they do.

—*Tess Gallagher*

You have to be a little patient if you're an artist, people don't always get you the first time.

—*Kate Millet*

Audience

I often feel dismayed when I think that the only readers of poetry are other poets, for that implies a decadence — that the craft is so inbred that only a privileged few can understand it.

—*Diane Wakoski*

People, even very intellectual people, are afraid of poetry.

—*Rita Dove*

When you reach out and touch other human beings, it doesn't matter whether you call it therapy or teaching or poetry.

—*Audre Lorde*

I want my public to be the masses.

—*Gloria Fuertes*

What is important is whatever the reader sees, not what the writer thinks he put in it. . . . Words are symbols and all the associations they carry can't be controlled.

—*Shirley Ann Grau*

Audience

I love to sleep and I feel that my dreams are more interesting than my life. I would like the reader to have the same sense after reading a poem, that you have when you wake up from a dream so vivid you can't get rid of it.

—Diane Wakoski

The whole point is to have the characters move off the page and inhabit the imagination of whoever has opened herself to them. I don't want to write books that you can close and walk off and read another one right away — like a television show, where you just flick the channel.

—Toni Morrison

You can't clobber any reader while he's looking. You divert his attention, then you clobber him and he never knows what hit him.

—Flannery O'Connor

I never think of my audience when I'm writing. If I did, it would be my mother and I'd never get a word on paper. I write to clarify for myself the realities I live in, and want to understand.

—Jane Rule

Audience

All poetry is confessional. The poet's self speaks to the reader's self, and though they are often separated by history, geography, and gender, there is no mistaking the pang, the shock, of kinship.

—Joyce Carol Oates

It is almost impossible to find a poet in the poetry world who will like your poetry if you tell him you do not like his.

—Diane Wakoski

I'm a lousy writer; a helluva lot of people have got lousy taste.

—Grace Metalious

Performance is an ideal way to deal with the problem of not having many personal relationships. A dilemma when you're not having relationships in depth is that you don't get used up enough, you don't get to really spring it, you know. I get to come out on stage and just pour everything I can think of into it. And then I walk away, and I haven't made a twenty-year commitment.

—Bobbie Louise Hawkins

Audience

Poetry is an oral tradition. I think it immensely enhances the person's poetry for an audience to hear it in the poet's voice.

—*Maxine Kumin*

A poem is not finished until I feel the flavor of the audience reaction rising up to me.

—*Audre Lorde*

Writers should be read, but neither seen nor heard.

—*Daphne Du Maurier*

The publishing industry is about twenty years behind the reading public.

—*Paula Gunn Allen*

There's nobody out there waiting for it, and nobody's going to scold you if you don't do it.

—*Lynne Sharon Schwartz*

Audience

The most moving form of praise I receive from readers can be summed up in three words: *I never knew.* Meaning, I see these people (call them Indians, Filipinos, Koreans, Chinese) around me all the time and I never knew they had an inner life.

—*Bharati Mukherjee*

I write what I most feel like reading, letting my enthusiasm as an eventual reader propel me through the first draft. My ideal book, could I but write it, would combine elements of Carolyn Keene, Kurt Vonnegut, Jr., Jane Austen, and Earle Stanley Gardner. It might not sell, but no one could accuse me of following a formula.

—*Lia Matera*

It's amazing the extent to which readers will think that everything that anybody in any of your books says is an expression of your own opinion. Literature just doesn't work like that.

—*Margaret Atwood*

I assure you I am not as good a writer as some of you may think I am. It is you and what you bring to it . . . the common work that we do together . . . all this is part of the making of style.

—*Tillie Olson*

Audience

I don't think American Indian literature should be distinguished from mainstream literature. Setting it apart and saying that people with special interest might read this literature sets Indians apart too.

—*Louise Erdrich*

When critics do not find what they expect, they cannot imagine that the fault may lie in their expectations.

—*Joanna Russ*

There is an expectation among readers and critics that I should represent the race. Each artist has a unique voice. Many readers don't understand that. What I look forward to is the time when many of us are published and then we will be able to see the range of viewpoints, of visions, of what it is to be Chinese-American.

—*Maxine Hong Kingston Olsen*

I write to get at the part of of people's emotional lives that they don't have control over, the part that can and will respond.

—*Ntozake Shange*

Poetry is emotion. What you want in making the poem is to deliver a feeling, and usually it's a complex feeling, but you want to have an impact, you want that intake of breath from the reader when you're finished.

—*Tess Gallagher*

Reading poetry is like having a lover. I mean, not everybody is suitable for everybody else, and it doesn't mean you are a bad lover because one person doesn't like to go to bed with you. You have to find the right person. I think that everybody has to find the right poetry.

—*Diane Wakoski*

If a woman be at liberty to write, let her write as if she were running a race in the sight of the world.

—*Mary Wilkins Freeman*

Beginning

Beginnings are apt to be shadowy.

—Rachel Carson

If you have any notion of where you are going, you will never get anywhere.

— Joan Miro

First thoughts have tremendous energy. It is the way the mind first flashes on something. The internal censor usually squelches them, so we live in the realm of second and third thoughts, thoughts on thoughts.

—Natalie Goldberg

It's not a bad idea to get in the habit of writing down one's thoughts. It saves one having to bother anyone with them.

—Isabel Colegate

I never write a synopsis or outline. If I did I might lose the idea before it was born.

—Elizabeth Jolley

Beginning

I so often begin in total chaos, not knowing *what* it is I'm doing, just knowing that I have this insistent rhythm, or I have this concept, that I want to fiddle around with. And it isn't until I get the poem out that I find out what it was saying, what I wanted to say.

—*Maxine Kumin*

The awakening of consciousness is not unlike the crossing of a frontier — one step and you are in another country.

—*Adrienne Rich*

Like an old gold-panning prospector, you must resign yourself to digging up a lot of sand from which you will later patiently wash out a few minute particles of gold ore.

—*Dorothy Bryant*

Once the grammar has been learned writing is simply talking on paper and in time learning what not to say.

—*Beryl Bainbridge*

Beginning

I'm always making little notes, false starts, beginnings. I wrote poetry for years before I ever wrote a story. I still work like a poet. Real slow.

—*Grace Paley*

I feel like I am just now learning how to write a poem. It has taken me over ten years to get to this point of just beginning.

—*Joy Harjo*

What's so hard about that first sentence is that you're stuck with it. Everything else is going to flow out of that sentence. And by the time you've laid down the first two sentences, your options are all gone.

—*Joan Didion*

I am certain before I begin writing a piece that I will not be able to put sentences together, or worse, that all I have to say has been said before, that there is no purpose, that there is no intrinsic authority to my own words.

—*Susan Griffin*

I can't write five words but that I change seven.

—*Dorothy Parker*

Beginning

When you write, don't say, "I'm going to write a poem." That attitude will freeze you right away. Sit down with the least expectation of yourself; say, "I am free to write the worst junk in the world."

—*Natalie Goldberg*

It's very hard to know, yourself, whether you're in a period of groping or in a period where the groping is rewarded by a creative outburst.

—*Marilynne Robinson*

I tend to wait for a poem to come to me. I feel that it is at least to some extent a mystical process, because when a poem is working, getting ready to be written, I know it. I know it with an absolute physical sureness.

—*Maxine Kumin*

I get rid of the garbage layer and then I can do the real work.

—*Paula Gunn Allen*

The misery of seeing the horrible chaos that actually precedes the creation of really first-rate work is so unnerving that most teachers of workshops would rather see the neat imitative poems.

—*Diane Wakoski*

Beginning

Those moments before a poem comes, when the heightened awareness comes over you, and you realize a poem is buried there somewhere, you prepare yourself. I run around, you know, kind of skipping around the house. It's as though I could fly, almost, and I get very tense before I've told the truth — hard. Then I sit down at the desk and get going with it.

—*Anne Sexton*

Had I been blessed with even limited access to my own mind there would have been no reason to write.

—*Joan Didion*

I have never written a book that was not born out of a question I needed to answer for myself.

—*May Sarton*

When I write first drafts I go on sheer drive, instinct, irresistible necessity, in the dark, until I can see where the poem is leading.

—*Heather McHugh*

Beginning

We are trying to make a vessel that won't break when the light comes in it, but also that isn't so dense that it won't conceal the light.

—*Deena Metzger*

The best time for planning a book is while you're doing the dishes.

—*Agatha Christie*

I start with a tingle, a kind of feeling of the story I will write. Then come the characters, and they take over, they make the story.

—*Isak Dineson*

The early stages of a novel are extremely painful; the first month or six weeks are terrible. It's a tremendous strain. I become insomniac; my mind is always working. In that stage I take notes anytime, even at midnight.

—*Joyce Carol Oates*

I began the novel *The Salt Eaters* the way a great many of my writings begin, as a journal entry.

—*Toni Cade Bambara*

Beginning

I began as a poet, writing poetry, I began to tell stories in the poems and then realized that there was not enough room in a poem.

—*Louise Erdrich*

What one story may have pointed out to me is of no avail in the writing of another.

—*Eudora Welty*

I suppose, at first, a writer's preoccupation tends to be with point of view, since you quickly learn that this is the most crucial and difficult choice you as the author have to make.

—*Diane Johnson*

I don't know what learning to write fiction means; I have the feeling I learned not to distract myself.

—*Marilynne Robinson*

I think the battle that one always has is the battle between inspiration and form.

—*Deena Metzger*

Beginning

Sometimes when you think you are done, it is just the edge of beginning. Probably that's why we decide we're done. It's getting too scary. We are touching down onto something real. It is beyond the point when you think you are done that often something strong comes out.

—*Natalie Goldberg*

A ratio of failures is built into the process of writing. The wastebasket has evolved for a reason. Think of it as the altar of the Muse Oblivion, to whom you sacrifice your botched first drafts, the tokens of your human imperfection.

—*Margaret Atwood*

There are a thousand ways to write, and each is as good as the other if it fits you, if you are any good.

—*Lillian Hellman*

Courage

I understand why a lot of writers drink heavily or shoot themselves. When you write, you tap the core of your wildness, you have to be prepared to let that live inside you and not destroy it.

—*Natalie Goldberg*

Everyone has talent. What is rare is the courage to follow the talent to the dark place it leads.

—*Erica Jong*

If we had to say what writing is, we would have to define it essentially as an act of courage.

—*Cynthia Ozick*

The battle is to hold to the vision I know I must express, but the confidence to do it, where does that come from?

—*Honor Moore*

One must think like a hero to behave like a merely decent human being.

—*May Sarton*

Courage

In the bigger scheme of things the universe is not asking us to *do* something, the universe is asking us to *be* something. And that's a whole different thing.

—*Lucille Clifton*

In time of crisis, we summon up our strength. Then, if we are lucky, we are able to call every resource, every forgotten image that can leap to our quickening, every memory that can make us know our power. And this luck is more than it seems to be: it depends on the long preparation of the self to be used.

—*Muriel Rukeyser*

Afraid is a country where they issue us passports at birth and hope we never seek citizenship in any other country.

—*Audre Lorde*

What did it mean for a black woman to be an artist in our grandmother's time? It is a question with an answer cruel enough to stop the blood.

—*Alice Walker*

Courage

It's only in my country that I find people who voluntarily choose to put everything at risk —of the in their personal life. I mean to most of us, the whole business of falling in love is so totally absorbing, nothing else matters. It's happened to me. There have been times in my life when I put the person I was in love with far ahead of my work. I would lose interest. I wouldn't even care if the book was coming out. I'd forget when it was being published and I wouldn't worry about the reception it got because I was in such a state of anguish over some man. And yet the people I know who are committed to a political cause never allow themselves to be deflected by this sort of personal consideration or ambition.

—

Nadine Gordimer

It is far easier to act under conditions of tyranny than to think.
—Hannah Arendt

The hardest thing we are asked to do in this world is to remain aware of suffering, suffering about which we can do nothing.
—May Sarton

Courage

Every woman who writes is a survivor.

—Tillie Olson

It isn't for the moment you are struck that you need courage, but for the long uphill climb back to sanity and faith and security.

—Anne Morrow Lindbergh

Life shrinks or expands according to one's courage.

—Anais Nin

To me real courage is metaphysical and has to do with keeping one's passion for life intact, one's curiosity at full stretch, when one is daily hemmed in by death, disease, and lesser mayhems of the heart.

—Diane Ackerman

The only courage that matters is the kind that gets you from one minute to the next.

—Mignon McLaughlin

Courage

However confused the scene of our life appears, however torn we may be who now do face that scene, it can be faced, and we can go on to be whole.

—Muriel Ruckeyser

I know I had to risk more in life before I could risk more in poetry.
—Shirley Kaufman

In the time of the poem it is still possible to find courage for the present moment.

—Tess Gallagher

The ability to live with fear is a part of the artist's condition. The fear of isolation can make a person choose not to make art.

—Bobbie Louise Hawkins

There's a lack of self-confidence that gets instilled very early in many young girls, before writing is even seen as a possibility. You need a certain amount of nerve to be a writer, an almost physical nerve, the kind you need to walk a log across a river.

—Margaret Atwood

Courage

One of the marks of a gift is to have the courage of it.
—*Katherine Anne Porter*

Originality does demand courage, the courage to become a person who is able to know his or her experience deeply, who is willing to feel and to question feeling, to dig for what the truth of a moment is, including the truth that may contradict external fact.
—*Jane Hirshfield*

I have found over the years that my writing has more courage than I do.

—*Linda Hogan*

Commitment

Writing is the only thing that, when I do it, I don't think I should be doing something else.

—*Gloria Steinem*

My dad's thing always was, if you are going to write, you sit down every single day or five days a week, whatever you are going to commit to, and you write, and you practice it like you practice piano scales, and you are bound to get better.

—*Anne Lamont*

I actually believe that most of life is probably an obstacle to writing for any writer. The world just does not need your gratuitous product. You must never quit insisting.

—*Jan Clausen*

How much it takes to become a writer. Bent (far more common than we assume), circumstances, time, development of craft — but beyond that: how much conviction as to the importance of what one has to say, one's right to say it.

—*Tillie Olson*

Commitment

Writing takes so much determination — you would do it on a rock in the middle of the ocean, if you had to.

—*Judy Grahn*

As I am a poet I express what I believe, and I fight against whatever I oppose, in poetry.

— *June Jordan*

For me writing is an incredible privilege. When I sit down at the desk, there are other women who are hungry, homeless. I don't want to forget that, that the world of matter is still there to be reckoned with. I feel a responsibility to other humans, and to the animal and plant communities as well.

—*Linda Hogan*

A striking characteristic of contemporary political poetry is that, more than in the past, it is written by people who are active participants in the causes they write about, and not simply observers.

—*Denise Levertov*

Commitment

You will never be better than your own judgement, and you will never be satisfied with what you do. Ambition will, and should always outstrip achievement.

—Fay Weldon

I know well enough that very few people who are supposedly interested in writing are interested in writing well.

—Flannery O'Connor

A writer must be willing to sit at the bottom of the pit, commit herself to stay there, and let all the wild animals approach, even call them up, then face them, write them down, and not run away.

—Natalie Goldberg

To say, "Well, I write when I really get into it" is a bunch of bull. Put the paper in the typewriter, stare at it a long time, get snowblindness if you have to, but write something.

—Erma Bombeck

If I've done my two or three pages (which is my output when I'm working on a novel), I know that I'll feel good the rest of the day.

—Erica Jong

Commitment

The life inside my poems was worth whatever it took to get there: guilt and compromise, tenacity, an inner secrecy that hid behind the facade of suburban housewife, Girl Scout leader, swimming instructor, chauffeur, and straw boss.

—Maxine Kumin

You can aim for what you want and if you don't get it, you don't get it but if you don't aim you don't get anything.

—Francine Prose

I saw myself sitting in the crotch of this fig tree, starving to death, just because I couldn't make up my mind which of the figs I would choose. I wanted each and every one of them, but choosing one meant losing all the rest, and, as I sat there, unable to decide, the figs began to wrinkle and go black, and, one by one, they plopped to the ground at my feet.

—Sylvia Plath

I would never encourage anyone to be a writer. It's too hard. It's just too hard to do.

—Eudora Welty

Commitment

If I just work when the spirit moves me, the spirit will ignore me.
—*Carolyn Forche*

I feel strongly that I have a responsibility to all the sources that I am: to all past and future ancestors, to my home country, to all places that I touch down on and that are myself, to all voices, all women, all of my tribe, all people, all earth, and beyond that to all beginnings and endings.
—*Joy Harjo*

And the trouble is, if you don't risk anything, you risk even *more*.
—*Erica Jong*

Writing has not become easier after all these years. It is harder — perhaps because of the standards you set for your work.
—*Elizabeth Hardwick*

Discipline doesn't come into it. It is what one has to do. The impulse is stronger than anything.
—*Edna O'Brien*

Commitment

In order to do creative work in any of the arts or sciences you must go through long or short spells of not knowing what is going on, of being irritated, and not being able to find the cause, of being willing to work as hard as you can and what happens isn't valuable enough, isn't good enough, isn't what you meant to do, what you meant to say. Then, if you can bear it, if you don't quit and move to Canada or call up Joe and go hiking for two weeks or quit your job or get a divorce or do anything else to relieve the pain, and it is pain, it's really irritating, it puts you in a bad mood, you are irritable to children and can't focus on anything and keep changing your mind, if you can put up with it and just go right on sitting down at that desk every day no matter how much it seems to be an absurd and useless and boring thing to do, the good stuff will suddenly happen.

—Ellen Gilchrist

Nothing seems to me to involve more intellectual effort than the organizing of a big novel, and I cannot imagine anything more rewarding.

—Joyce Carol Oates

All writers write "in spite of."

—Lisa Alther

Craft

Craft is a trick you make up to let you write the poem.

—*Anne Sexton*

Writing is more than just the making of a series of comprehensible statements: it is the gathering in of connotations, the harvesting of them, like blackberries in a good season, ripe and heavy, snatched from among the thorns of logic.

—*Fay Weldon*

Make the familiar exotic; the exotic familiar.

—*Bharati Mukherjee*

There are many poets from Byron to the present who accept the romantic notion that equates spontaneity with poetic genius. Your first impulse is so wonderful you don't do anything to it. In the words of a student I had at Stanford "that would violate the integrity of the poem." But what you try to do with revision is to find the integrity of the poem.

—*Carolyn Kizer*

Craft

I see my ideas as something like the blocks of marble in which Michaelangelo's Slaves were trapped: I believe somehow that the form is in there, imminent, only trapped, and I can't give up until I find it.

—*Rosellen Brown*

If technique is of no interest to a writer, I doubt that the writer is an artist.

—*Marianne Moore*

Think of everything you write as material you can always use later. Don't be afraid to cut just because you love something.

—*Amy Hempel*

You build a novel the same way you do a pyramid. One word, one stone at a time, underneath a full moon when the fingers bled.

—*Kate Braverman*

Craft

I might write four lines or I might write twenty. I subtract and I add until I really hit something I want to do. You don't always whittle down, sometimes you whittle up.

—*Grace Paley*

I cross out all the words except those that affect me deeply, those for which I have some "irrational" love. I keep those and build again. And again. All the while knowing that deeper meaning will rise to the surface like the form in a piece of stone, or the grain of a polished wood, if I have faith in this knowledge inside me.

—*Susan Griffin*

Poetry is the most frustrating and demanding of the written arts because every single word must fit as perfectly as possible for the poem to go. With fiction you have a few to throw away.

—*Laurel Speer*

The dry twigs left of a vanished life, whatever its fullness once was, are rubbed together until they catch fire.

—*Patricia Hampl*

Craft

People say, "You're writing fiction. What do you do research for? Why don't you just make it up?" Well, in a work of fiction, even if it's a modern novel set in Washington, D.C., if you're going to mention the address of the White House, you'd better have that address right. Because if all the basic facts that you put down are as accurate as you can get them, it aids readers in suspending their sense of disbelief.

—*Jean M. Auel*

I usually work it over and beat it up and sling it around the room a lot before I get to the typing stage. I hate to type — hate, hate — so things get cut mercilessly at that stage.

—*Toni Cade Bambara*

First draft is usually slow murder and each succeeding draft has more play, more bounce, more light in it.

—*Marge Piercy*

You do not create a style. You work and develop yourself; your style is an emanation from your own being.

—*Katherine Anne Porter*

Craft

I am governed by the pull of a sentence as the pull of a fabric is governed by gravity. I like the end-stopped line and dislike the reversed order of words, like symmetry.

—*Marianne Moore*

I spend most of my writing life revising. I seem to work in layers. So a chapter or a story doesn't really find its shape and emphasis, its color, until the fifth or sixth draft, and I do many more revisions just to polish the stones.

—*Mona Simpson*

For me, there are two very basic and different processes for revising my poetry. One is recognizing that a poem has not yet become itself. In other words, I mean that the feeling, the truth that the poem is anchored in is somehow not clearly clarified inside of me, and as a result it lacks something. Then it has to be re-felt. Then there's the other process which is easier. The poem is itself, but it has rough edges that need to be refined. That kind of revision involves picking the image that is more potent or tailoring it so that it carries the feeling.

—*Audre Lorde*

Craft

So many of my poems will go through thirty-five or forty different permutations. It's not at all unusual for me.

—*Maxine Kumin*

Writing for me is a ragged and restless activity with scattered fragments to be pieced together rather like a patchwork quilt.

—*Elizabeth Jolley*

Novice writers, even when they get a good dialogue style, frequently have everybody talking the same way. If they didn't identify the speaker, the reader wouldn't know. You've got to be able to distinguish among your characters.

—*Toni Morrison*

I simply cannot stand he-said/she-said any more.

—*Nadine Gordimer*

The hardest thing for me is getting people in and out of rooms — the mechanics of a story.

—*Eudora Welty*

Craft

I don't have a very clear idea of who the characters are until they start talking. Then I start to love them. By the time I finish the book, I love them so much that I want to stay with them.

—*Joan Didion*

I believe I have a tendency to go too far with endings, and someone always talks me out of the last little sting in the tail I had planned.

—*Diane Johnson*

Tell almost the whole story.

—*Anne Sexton*

I love closure. Especially in any kind of writing. I like to tie off the tale with some statement that sounds as though nothing further can be said.

—*Nancy Mairs*

Whenever I get lost in a novel I just throw a poem in. What it does is flare up, and it's so illuminated that I'm able to see where to go. I write between these illuminations.

—*Kate Braverman*

Craft

I always write my last lines, my last paragraph, my last page first, and then I go back and work towards it . . . . How I get there is God's grace.

—*Katherine Anne Porter*

There is such a thing as fussing too much; it can deaden the work. There is also such a thing as stopping too soon; this gives the work a kind of incompleteness that is more annoying than it is mysterious. Learning when "enough is enough" is the discipline of a lifetime.

—*Gail Godwin*

One way of ending the poem is to turn it back on itself, like a serpent with its tail in its mouth.

—*Maxine Kumin*

In your own heart, if you are a poet, you know which of your poems came out of the blood of your life, and you also know that you worked hardest to make them your most beautiful poems too, because they meant so much to you. No critic needs to tell you when you are writing something powerful.

—*Diane Wakoski*

Love

Love is the extremely difficult realization that something other than oneself is real.

—*Iris Murdoch*

The eskimos had fifty-two names for snow because it was important to them: there ought to be as many for love.

—*Margaret Atwood*

In real love you want the other person's good. In romantic love you want the other person.

—*Margaret Anderson*

To fall in love you have to be in the state of mind for it to take, like a disease.

—*Nancy Mitford*

Love has always been the motivating force in my life.

—*Kathleen Fraser*

Love

For women, the only sane way to live through a romance is to live through it without closure. Marriage to a lover is fatal; lovers are not husbands. More important, husbands are not lovers. The compulsion to find a lover and husband in a single person has doomed more women to misery than any other illusion.

—Carolyn Heilburn

Love is purely a creation of the human imagination . . . the most important example of how the human imagination continually outruns the creature it inhabits.

—Katherine Anne Porter

In a great romance, each person plays a part that the other really likes.

—Elizabeth Ashley

I am a woman trying to understand love. I am trying to understand how the uprooting exhilaration of the first months of expressed passion can become, in a short period of time, the source of pain, of loss of self.

—Jane Lazarre

Love

If only one could tell true love from false love as one can tell mushrooms from toadstools.

—*Katherine Mansfield*

Anxiety is love's greatest killer. It makes one feel as you might when a drowning man holds onto you. You want to save him, but you know he will strangle you with his panic.

—*Anais Nin*

No temptation can ever be measured by the value of its object.

—*Colette*

Love poems, particuliarly, are elegies because if we were not informed with a sense of dying we wouldn't be moved to write love poems. The best love poems have that element of longing in them: that either they'll lose that love or that time will take it away.

—*Maxine Kumin*

No matter what the subject, the subject is always love.

—*Ingrid Bengis*

Love

Just how difficult it is to write biography can be reckoned by anybody who sits down and considers just how many people know the real truth about his or her love affairs.

—*Rebecca West*

Whenever one of us falls in love our friends watch it as they would the progress of a disease.

—*Ellen Gilchrist*

It is only necessary to know that love is a direction and not a state of the soul. If one is unaware of this, one falls into despair at the first onslaught of affliction.

—*Simone Weil*

The more you love someone the more he wants from you and the less you have to give since you've already given him your love.

—*Nikki Giovanni*

No partner in a love relationship should feel that she has to give up an essential part of herself to make it viable.

—*May Sarton*

Love

I do not understand my relations with men. I have searched for love, yet always find those men who cannot love. These are the ones I care for with a deep passion. And the others, those who could love me, I mold into friends. I know I am not the only woman in the world who does this. I know many women who do the same.

—*Mary Morris*

You mustn't force sex to do the work of love or love to do the work of sex.
—*Mary McCarthy*

Love, love, love — all the wretched cant of it, masking egotism, lust, masochism, fantasy under a mythology of sentimental postures, a welter of self-induced miseries and joys, blinding and masking the essential personalities in the frozen gestures of courtship, in the kissing and the dating and the desire, the compliments and the quarrels which vivify its barrenness.
—*Germaine Greer*

Love's a disease. But curable.

—*Rose Macauley*

Love

I have a strong suspicion, but I can't be sure, that much that passes for constant love is a golded-up moment walking in its sleep.

—*Zora Neale Hurston*

I wanted to write about love, but I didn't, and it's a damn good thing I didn't try because I didn't know how to do it at all.

—*Jessamyn West*

They sicken of the calm, who knew the storm.

—*Dorothy Parker*

The epiphany of orgasms or infatuations is a consistently sought after reward for leading an otherwise responsible life.

—*Ntozake Shange*

In my sex fantasy, nobody ever loves me for my mind.

—*Nora Ephron*

Love

Love that stammers, that stutters, is apt to be the love that loves best.

—*Gabriela Mistral*

A common practice is to insist on the need to be alone and unloved and unloving, as though the experience of love is too tawdry and human, too diminishing and full of meaning, and that to participate in it is an indulgence and a flight from art.

—*Cynthia Kraman*

We left, as we have left all our lovers, as all lovers leave all lovers, much too soon to get the real loving done.

—*Judy Grahn*

Love doesn't just sit there, like a stone, it has to be made, like bread; remade all the time, made new.

—*Ursula K. Le Guin*

Pay attention to what they tell you to forget.

—*Muriel Ruckeyser*

Nothing is so good as it seems beforehand.

—*George Eliot*

We forget all too soon the things we thought we could never forget. We forget the loves and the betrayals alike, forget what we whispered and what we screamed, forget who we were.

—*Joan Didion*

Memory is a story we make up from snatches of the past.

—*Lynne Sharon Schwartz*

How uncanny to go back in memory to a house from which time has stolen all the furniture, and to find the one remembered chair, and write it so large, so deep, that it furnishes the entire vacant room.

—*Patricia Hampl*

Memory

The events of childhood do not pass, but repeat themselves like seasons of the year.

—Eleanor Farjeon

Words are more powerful than perhaps anyone suspects, and once deeply engraved in a child's mind, they are not easily eradicated.

—May Sarton

Perhaps it is our very forgetting that allows these past images significance. If we remembered constantly, the time fabric of our lives would remain whole and we would have no need of the poem to reinvolve us in what was a part of what is and may be.

—Tess Gallagher

It doesn't matter who my father was; it matters who I remember he was.

—Anne Sexton

What we remember is only a ripple in a pond.

—Nikki Giovanni

Memory

Most of the basic material a writer works with is acquired before the age of fifteen.

—*Willa Cather*

As a child I read more than I did, and so in many ways my memories are not only of real events but of books and of stories and of ideas.

—*Josephine Humphreys*

I remember stepping outside and seeing a large ship in the sky and not being too surprised, and thinking I wanted to share this with someone else. I went and got my mother, and by the time we got out there, the ship had gone on elsewhere. But she didn't in any way say, "Oh, you didn't see anything at all."

—*Nancy Willard*

You have to get to the point where you can open up the memories so you can get the spaces you can live with.

—*Carole Maso*

Memory

A theme may seem to have been put aside, but it keeps returning —
,the same thing modulated, somewhat changed in form.

—*Muriel Ruckeyser*

I can't know the best things I know until I write.

—*Leslie Marmon Silko*

Poems are like dreams; in them you put what you don't know you
know.

—*Adrienne Rich*

If you wake up in the morning with a great sense of the things that
have to be done in the day in order to get through to the next day,
you lose the sense of the day as any kind of end in itself.

—*Fay Weldon*

Perspective, I soon realized, was a fine commodity, but utterly
useless when I was in the thick of things.

—*Ingrid Bengis*

Memory

My memory is certainly in my hands. I can remember things only if I have a pencil and I can write with it and I can play with it.

—*Rebecca West*

You saw something on the bus, you overheard a snippet of dialogue on the bus and you start trying to recreate it, and pretty soon you are putting all the details in, and it's triggered your imagination and these old, old, thirty-year-old memories. . . . You remember who you were and then pretty soon you are just jamming and time is passing and you are just like a musician jamming.

—*Anne Lamont*

Writers live twice.

—*Natalie Goldberg*

The old folks say, "It's not how little we know that hurts so, but that so much of what we know ain't so."

—*Toni Cade Bambara*

Memory

I hate writing about my writing because I have nothing to say about it. I have nothing to say about it because I can't remember what goes on when I'm doing it. That time is like small pieces cut out of my brain.

—*Margaret Atwood*

Memory is neither factual or literal; we rewrite the past as we live the present.

—*Erica Jong*

How can a writer express what is most vital in her experience while anxiously watching her tongue lest she slip the wrong word?

—*Jan Clausen*

I am the kind of person who wakes up at four in the morning and suddenly thinks of what she should have said yesterday at lunch. For me, writing something down was the only road out.

—*Anne Tyler*

Memory

I can't seem to fictionalize in poetry the way some poets do. I tend to want to work with the actual experience, and to retell it in my own way, but to use those elements in a way that's fairly close to what happened.

—*Tess Gallagher*

Don't identify too strongly with your work. Stay fluid behind those black and white words. They are not you. They were a great moment going through you. A moment you were awake enough to write down and capture.

—*Natalie Goldberg*

I think the one lesson I have learned is that there is no substitute for paying attention.

—*Diane Sawyer*

Until we understand the assumptions in which we are drenched we cannot know ourselves.

—*Adrienne Rich*

Domestic Life

I was standing in the schoolyard waiting for a child when another mother came up to me. "Have you found work yet?" she asked. "Or are you still just writing?"

—*Anne Tyler*

How I think about my work is indistinguisable from the way I think about my needlepoint or cooking: here is the project I'm involved in. It is play. In this sense all my life is spent in play — sewing or needlepoint, or picking flowers or writing, or buying groceries.

—*Diane Johnson*

It's very difficult to be married and write, to be unmarried and write, to have children or not have children and write.

—*Laurel Speer*

I just flat out announce I'm working, leave me alone and get out of my face. When I "surface" again, I try to apply the poultices and patch up the holes I've left in relationships around me. That's as much as I know how to do . . . so far.

—*Toni Cade Bambara*

Domestic Life

For the seven years I was married my belief system was, "You only write when you're unhappy, and I'm happy; therefore, I don't have to write." So I lost seven years of my writing life doing other stuff.

—*Carolyn See*

The surest way to be alone is to get married.

—*Gloria Steinem*

I never married because there was no need. I have three pets at home which answer the same purpose as a husband. I have a dog which growls every morning, a parrot which swears all the afternoon and a cat that comes home late at night.

—*Marie Corelli*

When he is late for dinner and I know he must be either having an affair or lying dead in the street, I always hope he's dead.

—*Judith Viorst*

Domestic Life

It seemed to me that the desire to get married-which — I regret to say, I believe is basic and primal in women — is followed almost immediately by an equally basic and primal urge — which is to be single again.

—*Nora Ephron*

A woman at home is considered a housewife no matter what else she is doing. A man writing at home is a WRITER and often has a wife to bring him coffee and see he is well cared for and not disturbed. Whose duty is it to see that I am well cared for? Oh, I would love a wife.

—*Judy Blume*

Making the decision to have a child — it's momentous. It is to decide forever to have your heart go walking around outside your body.

—*Elizabeth Stone*

Because I am a mother, I am capable of being shocked: as I never was when I was not one.

—*Margaret Atwood*

Domestic Life

Another thing that seems quite helpful to the creative process is having babies. It does not detract at all from one's creativity. It reminds one that there is always more where that came from and there is never any shortage of ideas or of the ability to create.

—*Fay Weldon*

Once the children were in the house the air became more vivid and more heated; every object in the house grew more alive.

—*Mary Gordon*

The distillation of everyday life experiences is exactly what I am trying to particularize and order in poetry.

—*Maxine Kumin*

Writing about family life in the twentieth century may really mean writing about mothers and children. Fathers are present as absences in family life. Who really had a father? Even people who did have fathers didn't. Men were working.

—*Mona Simpson*

Domestic Life

I can't mate in captivity.

—*Gloria Steinem*

A successful parent is one who raises a child who grows up and is able to pay for her or his own psychoanalysis.

—*Nora Ephron*

The only thing that seems eternal and natural in motherhood is ambivalence.

—*Jane Lazarre*

Until I was twenty-eight I had a kind of buried self who didn't know she could do anything but make white sauce and diaper babies.

—*Anne Sexton*

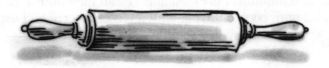

Domestic Life

People just don't think of writing seriously. If I had been going off to teach all day, it would have been different. They wouldn't interrupt your work if you were employed at a grocery store. That's considered serious business. It's because you work at home. People think they can interrupt writing.

—*Jessamyn West*

It's not the tragedies that kill us it's the messes. I can't stand messes.

—*Dorothy Parker*

The house has to be clean and in order because I have to be able to sift through the creative disorder in my mind. The mental disorder that I'm exploring has to bounce off the walls. It has to go in and out of different rooms. If the room is not in order, then I can't distinguish which is which, and that really drives me crazy.

—*Alexis DeVeaux*

I mutter and mumble. I get mad and I clean the house a lot and I pick fights with people. Living with a writer is terrible. I used to live with a writer so I know it's terrible.

—*Paula Gunn Allen*

Domestic Life

I am different from most women I know and run into every day, and the main difference is that I am totally incompetent in the household and I am extraordinarily messy. Clutter piles up around me, and I've been like that since I was twelve years old, and it's pathological. It's the kind of messiness that disgusts other people and I've never understood it. What's in my head is not a mess, but it's a vast amount of stuff. It's not ordered or clean, it's very confusing, but it's interesting and I like it that way and I certainly like to have a house that way. I like it to be full of surprise and disorder.

—*Josephine Humphreys*

My family can always tell when I'm well into a novel because the meals get very crummy.

—*Anne Tyler*

Gradually I began to reach the point when a line of poetry and a menu could be cooking in my head side by side, without interfering with one another.

—*Ruth Whitman*

Domestic Life

》—♡→

I got used to hearing stories and I realized that it wasn't so much what happened as who was doing the telling. All life seems to go on in the kitchen. So women have a chance to hear everyday speech with all the nuances and the unsaid, the between the lines of every-day speech.

—*Nancy Willard*

Forget the room of one's own — write in the kitchen, lock yourself up in the bathroom. Write on the bus or the welfare line, on the job or during meals, between sleeping or waking. While you wash the floor or clothes listen to the words chanting in your body.

—*Gloria Anzaldua*

Sometimes the only quiet and private place where I could write a sonnet was in the bathroom, because that was the only room where the door could be locked and no one would intrude.

—*Margaret Walker*

A mother is neither cocky, nor proud, because she knows the school principal may call at any minute to report that her child has just driven a motorcycle through the gymnasium.

—*Mary Kay Blakely*

Domestic Life

There is still the sense that "it's very nice that you're writing your little stories but you really shouldn't neglect your children to write those stories." Men don't have to do that. If they choose to put their pens down and go look after the kids, it's because they feel like doing it.

—*Alice McDermott*

Any mother could perform the jobs of several air-traffic controllers with ease.

—*Lisa Alther*

House ordering is my prayer, and when I have finished, my prayer is answered. And bending, stooping, scrubbing, purifies my body as prayer doesn't.

—*Jessamyn West*

Even St. Teresa said, "I can pray better when I'm comfortable," and she refused to wear her haircloth shirt or starve herself. I don't think living in cellars and starving is better for an artist than it is for anybody else.

—*Katherine Anne Porter*

Education

Distance, then, was what I was to strive for. Distance from the body, from the heart, but most of all, distance from the self as writer. I could never understand exactly what they meant or how to do it; it was like trying to follow the directions on a home permanent in 1959.

—*Mary Gordon*

The damage done to women writers in their adolescence and young womanhood by reading about the poet "he"— all references to artists being put in masculine terms, as if there wasn't any such thing as a woman writer — is so damaging.

—*Carolyn Kizer*

Prejudices, it is well known, are most difficult to eradicate from the heart whose soil has never been loosened or fertilized by education; they grow there, firm as weeds among stones.

—*Charlotte Bronte*

Poems are taught as though the poet has put a secret key in his words and it is the reader's job to find it. Poems are not mystery novels.

—*Natalie Goldberg*

Education

I think we, Black women specifically, have an enormous literary tradition and have knowledge of it and there is this pretense that we should be downwardly mobile to reach everybody which I don't think is necessary. I find it very much like economic downward mobility which I don't particularly care for either. Once you have the privilege, if you want to reject it that's fine, but if you've worked hard for your education it doesn't make much sense.

—*Michelle Cliff*

Moralism is the set of rules learned by rote that keeps women locked in, so that intelligence can never meet the world head on.

—*Andrea Dworkin*

Good fiction is not preaching. If a writer is trying hard to convince you of something, then he or she should stick to nonfiction.

—*Terry McMillan*

I don't believe in craft. I always tell my students never, never, never take another creative writing course. It's most destructive. What is the use of obeying the rules, following the textbooks, if your voice doesn't sound different from other people's voices?

—*Kay Boyle*

Education

I don't believe in teaching poetry at all, but that's what they want one to do. You see so many poems every week, you just lose all sense of judgement.

—*Elizabeth Bishop*

A good teacher can save you ten years. You can't teach creativity, you can't infuse people with psychic energy, and you certainly can't give them a good ear, which is a gift of God, but you can teach people critical distance, how to look at their own work objectively as if it had been written by somebody else.

—*Carolyn Kizer*

Many people know about camera angles now, but not so many know about sentences.

—*Joan Didion*

I no more thought of style or literary excellence than the mother who rushes into the street and cries for help to save her children from a burning house, thinks of the teachings of the rhetorician or the elocutionist.

—*Harriet Beecher Stowe*

Education

No one who hasn't lived the life of a semi-cripple knows how much that means. I think it was perhaps the most important thing that happened to me. It formed me, guided me, instructed me, helped me, and humiliated me. All these things at once. I've never gotten over it and I am aware of the force and power of it.

—Dorothea Lange

If I had to give young writers advice, I'd say don't listen to writers talking about writing.

—Lillian Hellman

In school we had spelling lessons — those horrible lists of words to memorize week after week, and the boring exercises geared to teach us how to use each word correctly. I would finish the exercises as quickly as possible; then I'd look around for something to occupy myself with until my classmates finished. So I would use that week's word list to write a little story.

—Rita Dove

It seems to me that a great majority of academia who are dealing with what they call creative writing are very specifically creating a culture for themselves that will sustain *them*.

—Ntozake Shange

Education

Writing has become a career track. It's like going to law school or medical school. "I'll graduate, I'll go to writing school, I'll come out a writer." They come out and they think they're writers. I'm of the old school. Writers work, suffer, sit in cafes, talk to their friends — they live — and you become a writer alone. *You make yourself a writer.*

—*Lynne Sharon Schwartz*

I tend to be terribly bored by the writing of white academic poets. Hopelessly bored. I really don't care how many sex fantasies they had watching a bird on a fence. If you'll pardon the phrase I think in academia, in English departments, that the writers are just masturbating.

—*Wendy Rose*

There are certain forms of literature that the in-vogue sensibility doesn't want to deal with. It's like racism and sexism. When we say "it's like poetry," we are saying we don't really have to look at it, it's not important or really that serious.

—*Kate Braverman*

I try to tell people from the sciences: you know, don't get upset, don't demand to follow it in a logical step-by-step. Just keep reading it. Relax.

—*Leslie Marmon Silko*

Education

In many ways writing is the act of saying *I*, of imposing oneself upon other people, of saying *listen to me, see it my way, change your mind*. It's an aggressive, even hostile act.

—*Joan Didion*

I'm not a critic of my own work. It's not what I'm supposed to be about. I think literary analysis gives academics something to do.

—*Nikki Giovanni*

Everywhere I go I'm asked if I think the university stifles writers. My opinion is that they don't stifle enough of them.

—*Flannery O'Connor*

To me it's inconceivable that anyone should publish in their twenties unless they are Keats. I think it should be outlawed. They simply don't know enough.

—*Lynne Sharon Schwartz*

Education

I didn't miss a beat turning down a scholarship at a Catholic college where I had been assured I would get more "individual attention." Who wanted individual attention? I wanted to be left alone to lose my soul.

—*Patricia Hampl*

Education

For me, self-knowledge could only begin because there was a feminist movement.

—*Susan Griffin*

Thirty years ago, the average person in the street wouldn't have anything to do with a poet. Now I teach poetry to policemen.

—*Audre Lorde*

I grew up around boys who carried horn cases and girls who couldn't wait for their legs to grow and reach the piano pedals. I learned more from Bud Powell, Dizzy, Y'Bird, Miss Sassy Vaughn about what can be communicated, can be taught through structure, tone, metronomic, sense, and just sheer holy boldness than from any teacher of language arts. For the most part the voice of my work is bop.

—*Toni Cade Bambara*

The final lesson a writer learns is that everything can nourish the writer. The dictionary, a new word, a voyage, an encounter, a talk on the street, a book, a phrase learned.

—*Anais Nin*

Men

Men require a lot from women, and taking care of yourself as a person is a full-time job. If you're taking care of yourself and another grown person, something is taken from you. . . . I think they ought to become persons, and then they don't have to lean so heavily on the female that she loses part of her life.

—*Joyce Carol Thomas*

I have yet to hear a man ask for advice on how to combine marriage and a career.

—*Gloria Steinem*

The trouble was, I hated the idea of serving men in any way.

—*Sylvia Plath*

Men have been taught to deal only with what they understand. This is what they respect. They know that somewhere feeling and knowledge are important, so they keep women around to do their feeling for them, like ants do aphids.

—*Audre Lorde*

Men

Beware of men who cry. It's true that men who cry are sensitive to and in touch with feelings, but the only feelings they tend to be sensitive to and in touch with are their own.

—*Nora Ephron*

I've never gone anywhere where the men have come up to my infantile expectations.

—*Rebecca West*

She was created to be the toy of man, his rattle, and it must jingle in his ears whenever, dismissing reason, he chooses to be amused.

—*Mary Wollstonecraft*

Philosopher: A man up in a balloon, with his family and friends holding the ropes which confine him to earth and trying to haul him down.

—*Louisa May Alcott*

Personally, I think if a woman hasn't met the right man by the time she's 24, she may be lucky.

—*Jean Kerr*

Men

The man-woman thing is a boring subject. It's essentially a dead end. It's going to come down to one of two things: either you're going to take off your clothes or you're not.

—Nikki Giovanni

Women want mediocre men, and men are working hard to become as mediocre as possible.

—Margaret Mead

Once you know what women are like, men get kind of boring. I'm not trying to put them down, I mean I like them sometimes as people, but sexually they're dull.

—Rita Mae Brown

Even feminists can become handmaidens to incredibly powerful, incredibly important, egotistical, patriarchal men. Every feminine bone in their bodies disappears when they get around these men. They are great feminists, but when they get around these men they turn to Jello.

—Elizabeth Winthrop

Men

Men want the same thing from their writers that they want from their wives, a certain type of predictability.

—*Kate Braverman*

Woman is not deluded. She must create without these proud delusions of man, without megalomania, without schizophrenia, without madness. She must create that unity which man first destroyed by his proud consciousness.

—*Anais Nin*

Freud is the father of psychoanalysis. It has no mother.

—*Germaine Greer*

I speak of poetry as the revelation or distillation of experience, not the sterile word play that, too often, the white fathers distorted the word poetry to mean — in order to cover their desperate wish for imagination without insight.

—*Audre Lorde*

Men

I find myself staying away, on the whole, unless they have been recommended to me as an exception, from work by white men, because this work seems to need to blunt or even bludgeon the sensibilities of its audience. This is also true of work by women or blacks who imitate that white male contemporary tradition.

—*Susan Griffin*

The problem lies not in the male defined reality that women are deficient and cannot write, but in the male monopoly on reality.

—*Dale Spender*

I found that sometimes at women-only readings, men would dress up like women and come to my readings to hear me, which really astonished me. They would creep in in dresses.

—*Judy Grahn*

The Virgin is now appearing to a whole class of kids in Czechoslovakia; she sees them and they see her every day. The priests are saying, "This is bullshit." Some bureaucrat in the Vatican said about this, "I can't stand these pious women." These guys don't care because they are stuck with, "My dick is so long and red and it's such an amazing sight;" that's where they are.

—*Carolyn See*

Men

I like men to behave like men - strong and childish.

—*Francoise Sagan*

Men

I have been told by male but not by female critics that my work was "exquisite," "lovely," "like a watercolor." They, of course, were painting in oils.

—*Mary Gordon*

All standards seem to exist to obscure meaning. I just want to say what I mean. Poetry has been controlled by men for so long. They've set the standards, the criteria for what's a good poem. It's all a bunch of shit, academic wanderings.

—*Pat Parker*

Men writers aren't thought of as "men writers;" they are thought of as great writers. It would be fine if the men writers would be called "men writers." It just never comes up - "Updike or Bellow, he's a really great man writer." But we frequently hear," Margaret Atwood is a really incredible woman writer." I say what a crock of shit.

—*Anne Lamont*

Muse

I grew up as a female who heard voices.

—*Lucille Clifton*

A writer's imagination must be filled not just with literal truths, but with the unseen, the unknown whose shy presence is felt.

—*Gretel Ehrlich*

When we take an author seriously, we prefer to believe that her vision derives from her individual and subjective and neurotic, tortured soul — we like artists to have tortured souls — not from the world she is looking at.

—*Margaret Atwood*

The world of imagination in which the writer must live is constantly being invaded by the enemy, the mundane world.

—*Margaret Walker*

Only women stir my imagination.

—*Virginia Woolf*

Perversity is the muse of modern literature.

—*Susan Sontag*

Muse

Black people have the ability as a race to speak in tongues, to dream in tongues, to love in tongues.

—Alexis DeVeaux

The influence for a writer my age is the rock music of the sixties. This music has given me a sense of cadence and rhythm and a feeling that I am not writing but composing and what I do with words are riffs and improvisations.

—Kate Braverman

I need to pull an idea from my soul or my body every day.

—Gloria Fuertes

The impulse for much writing is homesickness. You are trying to get back home, and in your writing you are invoking that home, so you are assuaging the homesickness.

—Joan Didion

The desire for self-expression afflicts people when they feel there is something of themselves which is not getting through to the outside world.

—Fay Weldon

Muse

When I couldn't find the poems to express the things I was feeling, I started writing poetry.

—*Audre Lorde*

The creative mind is intelligence in action in the world.

—*Andrea Dworkin*

It is impossible to be stupid while listening to Bach.

—*Ellen Gilchrist*

I'm often asked while on the road, "How autobiographical is your work?" - the assumption being that it has to be. Sometimes the question springs from the racist assumption that creative writing and art are the domain of white writers. Sometimes the question surfaces from a class base, that only the leisured and comfortable can afford the luxury of imagination. Sometimes it stems from the fact that the asker is just some dull, normal type who cannot conceive of the possibilty that some people have imagination, though they themselves do not, poor things.

—*Toni Cade Bambara*

Muse

My stories come to me as cliches. A cliche is a cliche because it's worthwhile. Otherwise, it would have been discarded.

—*Toni Morrison*

I suppose I am a born novelist, for the things that I imagine are more vital and vivid to me than the things I remember.

—*Ellen Glasgow*

To imagine the unimaginable is the highest use of the imagination.

—*Cynthia Ozick*

Imagination has always had powers of resurrection that no science can match.

—*Ingrid Bengis*

In praise of overlap I might say that I often go in search of one thing and come back with another.

—*Maxine Kumin*

Muse

I learn that the writer's pen is a microphone held up to the mouths of ancestors and even stones of long ago. That once given permission by the writer — a fool, and so why should one fear? - horses, dogs, rivers, and yes, chickens can step forward and expound on their lives.

—Alice Walker

For a long stretch it didn't feel like writing. I felt I was just taking down what came rushing out.

—Mona Simpson

A piece of writing is the product of a series of explosions in the mind.

—Ellen Gilchrist

Writing about why you write is a funny business, like scratching what doesn't itch. Impulses are mysterious, and explaining them must be done with mirrors, like certain cunning sleight-of-hand routines.

—Patricia Hampl

Really serious writing does come out of anguish.

—Joyce Carol Oates

Muse

I've never enjoyed the company of people who believe that by living a "writerly" life, complete with rejection notices papering the walls, the writing will follow. I've never believed anyone can will the mind to create a thing of beauty. I like to think artistic creation starts in a more mysterious place . . .

—*Kaye Gibbons*

How far can a Greek goddess lead a Black poet?

—*Rita Dove*

I look upon literature as an art, and I believe that if you misuse it or abuse it, it will leave you. It is not a thing that you can nail down and use as you want. You have to let it use you, too.

—*Katherine Anne Porter*

Literature must spring from the deep and submerged humus of our life.

—*Meridel LeSueur*

The white fathers told us, "I think therefore I am," and the black mothers in each of us - the poets - whisper in our dreams, "I feel therefore I can be free."

—*Audre Lorde*

Resistance

Not out but through.

—Aniela Jaffe

At fifteen life had taught me undeniably that surrender, in its place, was as honorable as resistance, especially if one had no choice.

—Maya Angelou

Writing is so difficult that I often feel that writers, having had their hell on earth, will escape all punishment hereafter.

—Jessamyn West

Each day that I don't write I get more fragmented.

—Erica Jong

I hit my head against the wall because I don't want to know all the terrible things that I know about. I don't want to feel all these wretched things, but they're in me already. If I don't get rid of them, I'm not ever going to feel anything else.

—Ntozake Shange

Resistance

None of the writing is easy, but I no longer refuse to do it for fear that I'll fail to get it right. It can never be right, I know; it can only be done.

—*Nancy Mairs*

It's hard to fight an enemy who has outposts in your head.

—*Sally Kempton*

Stress is basically a disconnection from the earth, a forgetting of the breath. Stress is an ignorant state. It believes that everything is an emergency. Nothing is that important. Just lie down.

—*Natalie Goldberg*

All writers have periods when they stop writing, when they cannot write, and this is always painful and terrible because writing is like breathing.

—*Audre Lorde*

Any writer who has difficulty in writing is probably not onto his true subject, but wasting time with false, petty goals; as soon as you connect with your true subject you will write.

—*Joyce Carol Oates*

Resistance

I work continuously within the shadow of failure. For every novel that makes it to my publisher's desk, there are at least five or six that died on the way.

—*Gail Godwin*

When you get into a tight place and everything goes against you, till it seems as though you could not hang on a minute longer, never give up then, for that is just the place and time that the tide will turn.

—*Harriet Beecher Stowe*

To oppose something is to maintain it.

—*Ursula K. LeGuin*

When I sit down in order to write, sometimes it's there; sometimes it's not. But that doesn't bother me anymore. I tell my students there is such a thing as "writer's block," and they should respect it. You shouldn't write through it. It's blocked because it ought to be blocked, because you haven't got it right now.

—*Toni Morrison*

Resistance

When we can begin to take our failures nonseriously, it means we are ceasing to be afraid of them.

—*Katherine Mansfield*

Why is what one longs to do such torture when one "has to" do it?

—*Rita Dove*

Not too long ago I tried to write a story. I got my name and address on the sheet; a title, which stank; and the first sentence: "The stranger appeared in the doorway." Then I had to lie down with a wet cloth on my face.

—*Dorothy Parker*

I do have to force myself, but once I get into it it's a pleasure. Why is it that it's so difficult when I know what a pleasure it will be? That's the question I'd most like answered.

—*Alix Kates Shulman*

There is no pleasure in having nothing to do; the fun is in having lots to do and not doing it.

—*Mary Little*

Resistance

In the face of an obstacle which is impossible to overcome, stubborness is stupid.

—Simone de Beauvoir

When a worker who knows how much more labor has to be done in no time nevertheless sits idle because caught in a situation where she can't work — visiting in a strange house overnight or eyes closed in the dentist's chair or darkness suddenly fallen deep in the woods — then the visions come assailing.

—Maxine Hong Kingston

Every poem, every page of fiction I have written, has been written with anxiety, occasionally panic, always uncertainty about its reception. Every life decision I have made — from changing jobs, to changing partners, to changing homes — has been taken with trepidation. I have not ceased being fearful, but I have ceased to let fear control me.

—Erica Jong

If you are not afraid of the voices inside you, you will not fear the critics outside you.

—Natalie Goldberg

Resistance

There's the blank page, and the thing that obsesses you. There's the story that wants to take you over and there's your resistance to it. There's your longing to get out of this, this servitude, to play hooky, to do anything else: wash the laundry, see a movie.

—*Margaret Atwood*

If you refuse to suffer the lesser madness you will have to suffer the greater madness.

—*Deena Metzger*

Everything is so dangerous that nothing is really very frightening.

—*Gertrude Stein*

I often find poetry frightening. I will go to lengths to avoid writing down lines that are forming in my mind. And when I am developing a poem, I must prevent one part of myself from finishing the poem in a quite conventional, predictable way before it is ready to be finished.

—*Susan Griffin*

Resistance

At times it seems hopeless, it's just not working. Those times I used to write anything and then throw it out, but that makes me crazy. Now I just have to wait — I haven't found the right door. I can't let it make me sick. All art is knowing when to stop.

—*Toni Morrison*

If you try and fail that's better than saying, I could have written it if I hadn't married Harold.

—*Carolyn See*

Silence

Silence never brought us anything.

—*Audre Lorde*

Writers are always afraid, "That was the last book. I'm through." You can have a year or two of feeling perfectly miserable. Usually what that means is that the well is filling back up and you can't get any water for a year or two.

—*Ursula K. Le Guin*

When I am not giving forth words, I am not certain any longer who I am.

—*Susan Griffin*

If we had a keen vision of all ordinary life, it would be like hearing the grass grow or the squirrel's heart beat, and we should die of the roar which lies on the other side of silence.

—*George Eliot*

Silence

We cannot speak of women writers in our century without speaking also of the invisible, the as innately capable: the born to the wrong circumstances, the diminished, the excluded, the lost, the silenced.

—Tillie Olson

Because society would rather we always wore a pretty face, women have been trained to cut off anger.

—Nancy Friday

Women will starve in silence until new stories are created which confer on them the power of naming themselves.

—Sandra Gilbert and Susan Gubar

If I dare add another voice to the din, it would be to plead for quietness — to ask that we learn to listen rather than to shout out, that most of all we heed the ones who are so oppressed they cannot speak at all.

—Joy Kogawa

Silence

When I didn't write I thought of making bombs and throwing them. Of shooting racists.

—Alice Walker

Writing helped me give voice to turn around a terrible silence that was killing me.

—Joy Harjo

The necessity for fiction was probably born of the problem of taboo on certain revelations.

—Anais Nin

A voice is a gift; it should be cherished and used, to utter fully human speech if possible. Powerlessness and silence go together.

—Margaret Atwood

I wasn't allowed to speak while my husband was alive, and since he's gone no one has been able to shut me up.

—Hedda Hopper

Silence

For generations women have been silenced in patriarchal order, unable to have their meanings encoded and accepted in the social repositories of knowledge.

—Dale Spender

Loneliness is never more cruel than when it is felt in close propinquity with someone who has ceased to communicate.

—Germaine Greer

People change and forget to tell each other.

—Lillian Hellman

It is not merely the fear of exposure that keeps me silent at times, but the fear of criticism that slides nastily over the work and becomes a moral damnation of myself or a condescending and reductive parlor psychoanalysis of my life.

—Jane Lazarre

Women have had the power of naming stolen from us.

—Mary Daly

Silence

The dominant reality would have us accept that it is difficult for women to write because they are *inferior,* not because they are women who have been denied access to the production of our cultural forms and are a *muted* group without a voice.

—*Dale Spender*

There is such a thing as silence — and the great, everpresent possibility that our poems may not get read.

—*Lorine Niedecker*

Who then tells a finer tale than any of us? Silence does.

—*Isak Dinesen*

A couple of poems I like a year look like a lot when they come out, but in fact are points of satisfaction separated by large vacancies.

—*Sylvia Plath*

Silence

I write poems about relationships, love relationships, and I'm not able to do that all the time. I could go two years without writing poems, and then write a dozen. Having a novel to work on, with the intricate puzzle of character and plot to work out, is satisfying for the time there is no poetry.

—*May Sarton*

If I don't have something to write on, it comes out of my mouth. It's got to come out one way or another.

—*Wendy Rose*

If I don't have anything to say for three or four months, I just don't write. When I read a book, I can always tell if the writer has written through a block. If he or she had just waited, it would have been better or different, or a little more natural. You can see the seams.

—*Toni Morrison*

I have to write. If I avoid that mandate, I wind up trying to kill myself. It's as simple as that.

—*Nancy Mairs*

Silence

I went through a period once when I felt like I was dying. I wasn't writing any poetry, and I felt that if I couldn't write I would split.

—*Audre Lorde*

When I'm not writing or planning some project in my head I'm depressed, or at least anxious and not terribly pleasant to be around.

—*Rosellen Brown*

Looking back, I imagine I was always writing. Twaddle it was too. But better far write twaddle or anything, anything, than nothing at all.

—*Katherine Mansfield*

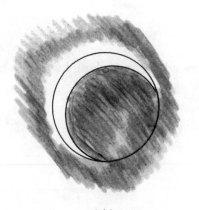

Spirituality

Words are the only "holy" for me. The only sanctity really, for me, is the sanctity of language.

—*Maxine Kumin*

The soul should always stand ajar, ready to welcome the ecstatic experience.

—*Emily Dickinson*

When we talk to God, we're praying. When God talks to us we're schizophrenic.

—*Lily Tomlin*

In church I fell in love with the rhythms of those who testified.

—*Joyce Carol Thomas*

If I were going to convert to any religion I would probably choose Catholicism because it at least has female saints and the Virgin Mary.

—*Margaret Atwood*

Spirituality

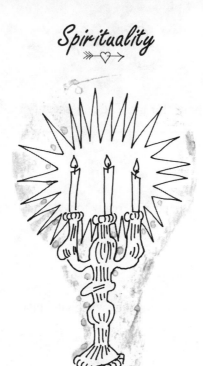

The act of writing is the act of making soul, alchemy.

—*Gloria Anzaldua*

My family was radically opposed to anything to do with literature. Although Ireland has produced so many great writers, there is a deep suspicion about writing there. Somehow they know that writing is dangerous, seditious, as in "In the beginning was the Word and the Word was with God and the Word *was* God."

—*Edna O'Brien*

Spirituality

Writing the poem is the poet's means of summoning the divine; the reader's may be through reading the poem, or through what the experience of the poem leads her to.

—*Denise Levertov*

Poetry has saved me again and again.

—*Muriel Rukeyser*

The problem was that, when Spirit came into the world, it came into the world, it came into the world in vessels which couldn't hold, contain the Spirit, and so they broke. And these divine sparks, which are broken bits of light, scattered all over the world.

—*Deena Metzger*

Put your ear down close to your soul and listen hard.

—*Anne Sexton*

For each of us as women, there is a dark place within where hidden and growing our true spirit rises.

—*Audre Lorde*

Spirituality

The world's spiritual geniuses seem to discover universally that the mind's muddy river, this ceaseless flow of trivia and trash, cannot be dammed, and that trying to dam it is a waste of effort that might lead to madness.
—Annie Dillard

I don't write poetry for content, but to articulate a sense, an intuition. I write a poem as an act of faith, an act of discovery. I don't experience poetry as self-expression or as therapy but as a conversation between me and the universe, the Spirit people, my guides, my own inner self.
—Paula Gunn Allen

Poetry answers a need cried out for from an unknown part of our souls.
—Susan Griffin

What they should be saying at these schools, rather than correcting technical flaws, is — do something with your spirit and your relationship to the universe.
—Lynne Sharon Schwartz

Religion and art spring from the same root and are close kin.
—Willa Cather

Spirituality

Spirituality necessitates certain kinds of political action. If you believe that the earth, and all living things, and all the stones are sacred, your responsibility really is to protect those things.

—*Linda Hogan*

What would have been the effect upon religion if it had come to us through the minds of women?

—*Charlotte Perkins Gilman*

All of us are all of us. All the great spirits of history are being reborn as women.

—*Lucille Clifton*

I'm not a naturalist in the activist sense of the word, though perhaps writing with a feeling of the sacred about a place is a kind of activism. Part of what you're doing as a writer is to make that silent language of mountains and trees and water part of your language. It's speaking all the time and I hear it speaking.

—*Tess Gallagher*

We tend to think of the erotic as an easy, tantalizing sexual arousal. I speak of the erotic as the deepest life force, a force which moves us toward living in a fundamental way.

—*Audre Lorde*

The secret of seeing is to sail on solar wind. Hone and spread your spirit, till you yourself are a sail, whetted, translucent, broadside to the merest puff.

—*Annie Dillard*

For me, writing is very much a spirtual practice. You have to sit there or stand there or be there, and be with the work. You are utterly in its service, and what you are trying to do is render this moment so that things are in perfect balance — make the vessel that the gods can come and sit in.

—*Deena Metzger*

When you respond to something because it's so beautiful, you're really looking at the soul of the person who made it.

—*Alice Walker*

It is the creative potential itself in human beings that is the image of God.

—*Mary Daly*

Truth

The basic problem that we have had was believing somebody else's story about us.

—*Luisah Teish*

What's terrible is to pretend that the second-rate is first rate. To pretend that you don't need love when you do; or you like your work when you know quite well you're capable of better.

—*Doris Lessing*

When one is pretending the entire body revolts.

—*Anais Nin*

I guess my tirades are always against some form of hypocrisy; some easy way of looking at the world. Some simplistic, sentimental approach to life.

—*Diane Wakoski*

We've become a society of screens, of layers that keep us from knowing the truth, as if the truth were unbearable; too much for us to deal with — like our feelings. So we deal with things through replications, through copying, through screens, through facsimiles, through fiction and faction.

—*Lynn Hershman*

Truth

Nobody will tell you the truth. You have to listen and you have to look because no one is going to tell you.

—*Audre Lorde*

But in order "not to know," large groups of people, whole nations, have to find a way to blunt their intelligence. A way must be found not to know. The cost must be enormous. People must deny over and over the intelligence of their senses. It is a denial of the most ancient poetic intelligence. It is a denial of reality. At its most extreme, it is madness.

—*Patricia Hampl*

There are no new truths, but only truths that have not been recognized by those who have perceived them without noticing.

—*Mary McCarthy*

Women have always been faced with encoded messages.

—*Nancy Willard*

Truth

It is neither cavalier nor a question of personal pathology, this compulsion in women writers, in women in general, to say what has been the unsayable, to write and speak of the bloody Kotex, the joy of masturbation, the incestuous desire, the feeling of submissive abandon or of a paralyzing, dry indifference during sex.

—Jane Lazarre

At the end *truth* is the only thing *worth having* : it's more thrilling than love, more joyful and more passionate.

—Colette

Only friends will tell you the truths you need to hear to make your life bearable.

—Francine Du Plessix Gray

I've done more harm by the falseness of trying to please than by the honesty of trying to hurt.

—Jessamyn West

Truth

If you want to write the truth, you must write about yourself. I am the only real truth I know.

—Jean Rhys

My responsibility to myself, my neighbors, my family and the human family is to try to tell the truth. That ain't easy. There are so few truth-speaking traditions in this society in which the myth of "Western civilization" has claimed the allegiance of so many.

—Toni Cade Bambara

A poem may know the subtlest elisions of feeling, the earliest signs of some pattern or discord.

—Diane Ackerman

Simply to speak the truth heals. The blood of the wound heals the wound.

—Susan Griffin

Artistic growth is, more than it is anything else, a refining of the sense of truthfulness. The stupid believe that to be truthful is easy; only the artist, the great artist, knows how difficult it is.

—Willa Cather

Truth

The passion for truth requires of us that we overcome one of the two great obstacles we face as writers, which is the fear of revealing the self.

—*Jane Hirshfield*

The artist who changes styles frequently is suspected from the start of all sorts of things but mostly, of not being sincere.

—*Cynthia Kraman*

Poetic truth is not necessarily autobiographical. It is truth that goes beyond the immediate self, another life.

—*Anne Sexton*

Some truths are better expressed through fiction than non-fiction. That's what storytelling is all about. A story bypasses the whole rational machinery of the brain — which so easily turns things around backward — and goes straight to the heart.

—*Kathryn Harrison*

In the first place all fiction ought to be true.

—*Mary Wilkins Freeman*

Truth

Most adults, having somehow lost touch with the great simplicities, have forgotten that to write is to speak of one's beliefs.

—*Kay Boyle*

The only time I know that something is true is at the moment I discover it in the act of writing.

—*Jean Malaquais*

You can't have three people looking over your shoulder, and you have to make sure not to censor yourself. You have to be willing to be seen as a jackass and a fool. You have to be willing to be wrong and you have to be risky. You have to take a certain amount of abuse, and the reason you're willing to do that is because you love the truth.

—*Grace Paley*

First and foremost I write for myself. I try to stay honest through pencil and paper. I run off at the mouth a lot. I've a penchant for flamboyant performance. I exaggerate to the point of hysteria.

—*Toni Cade Bambara*

Truth

Aesthetics, like philosophy and science, is invented not so much to enable us to get closer to reality as for the purpose of warding it off, of protecting against it.

—*Christa Wolf*

I tore myself away from the safe comfort of certainties through my love for truth; and truth rewarded me.

—*Simone de Beauvoir*

Cynicism is an unpleasant way of saying the truth.

—*Lillian Hellman*

Be critical. Women have the right to say: This is surface, this falsifies reality, this degrades.

—*Tillie Olson*

Eighty percent of the language lies to us . . . the language of diplomacy, politics, advertising . . . all the language of persuasion.

—*Deena Metzger*

Truth

One thing I've learned. Speech is far more guarded than talking through one's fingers.

—*Cynthia Ozick*

Speaking one's mind, after all, does not necessarily mean one is in touch with the truth or even with the facts.

—*Toni Cade Bambara*

It always comes back to the same necessity: go deep enough and there is a bedrock of truth, however hard.

—*May Sarton*

Women's art must be useful to women, must work in our interest. Must not work to divide us further, must not lie about us to each other, must not give false information which would fall apart when people try to make use of it.

—*Judy Grahn*

Writer's Life

My business is Circumference.

—*Emily Dickinson*

I want to say without sounding pompous that to me writing is life, that is, it is my way of being most fully alive, my central act of being; so then like life, sometimes it's easy and lovely; sometimes it's hard, sometimes it's impossible.

—*Ursula K. LeGuin*

I think that in order to write really well and convincingly, one must be somewhat poisoned by emotion.

—*Edna Ferber*

Writing is a part of my life; cooking is a part of my life. Making love is a part of my life; walking down the street is a part of it. Writing demands more time, but it takes from all these other activities.

—*Maya Angelou*

Poetry is not my life. My life is my life. Poetry is very big in my life and if poetry was gone from it, there would be space I don't know how I would fill. But if what you do is your life, that's tricky.

—*Lucille Clifton*

I finally figured out the only reason to be alive is to enjoy it.

—*Rita Mae Brown*

Life's a rash, and then there's death and the itching's over.

—*Cynthia Kraman*

I think I alternate between optimism and anxiety. I realize that should either of these get out of hand I would probably need a clever doctor.

—*Elizabeth Jolley*

How does one define one's own sense of being alive? I think it is this hum, or buzz, blablablablabla, that keeps on talking inside one's head. A stream of babble. The inner voice that never, never, never shuts up.

—*Cynthia Ozick*

Writer's Life

My lifetime listens to yours.

—*Muriel Ruckeyser*

Poetry is not only what is written in the poetry capitals of the world. Everywhere people write down words in an attempt to celebrate, mourn, or simply notice their own lives and what lies beyond their small spheres.

—*Judith Tannenbaum*

How hard it is to escape from places! However carefully one goes, they hold you — you leave little bits of yourself fluttering on the fences, little rags and shreds of your very life.

—*Katherine Mansfield*

The world I create in the writing compensates for what the real world does not give me.

—*Gloria Anzaldua*

All my work, my life, everything is about survival.

—*Maya Angelou*

Writer's Life

It is easier to live through someone else than to become complete yourself.

—*Betty Friedan*

We women have lived too much with closure: If he notices me, if I marry him, if I get into college, if I get this work accepted, if I get that job - there always seems to loom the possibility of something being over, settled, sweeping clear the way for contentment. This is the delusion of a passive life.

—*Carolyn G. Heilbrun*

I think I'm really not interested in the quest for the self anymore. It's absolutely useless to look for it, you won't find it, but it's possible in some sense to make it.

—*Mary McCarthy*

For twenty-five years I have been unlearning what I learned in my first twenty-five years.

—*Lynne Sharon Schwartz*

Writer's Life

I write. I rewrite. I lecture. I teach. I review. I edit. I perform. I don't watch television. I don't read a newspaper. I don't read magazines. I have few conventional pastimes. I have to protect myself from the toxicity of this culture. I read poetry out loud every day. I read my work out loud. I meditate.

—*Kate Braverman*

The most exhausting thing in my life is being insincere.

—*Anne Morrow Lindbergh*

You can live a lifetime and, at the end of it, know more about other people than you know about yourself.

—*Beryl Markham*

What you write comes out of how deeply you live your life.

—*Deena Metzger*

I wonder if the artist ever lives his life — he is so busy recreating it.

—*Anne Sexton*

Writer's Life

It's not the length but the quality of life that matters to me. It has always been important to me to write one sentence at a time, to live every day as if it were my last and judge it in those terms, often badly, not because it lacked grand gesture or grand passion but because it failed in the daily virtues of self-discipline, kindness, and laughter.

—*Jane Rule*

When you are a writer your senses never atrophy.

—*Phyllis A. Whitney*

Just being in a room with myself is almost more stimulation than I can bear.

—*Kate Braverman*

At no point have I ever been able successfully to keep a diary; my approach to daily life ranges from the grossly negligent to the merely absent.

—*Joan Didion*

I can't even keep a journal. I'm always losing the book. I have no discipline.

—*Grace Paley*

Writer's Life

I think I've only spent about ten percent of my energies on writing. The other ninety percent went to keeping my head above water.

—*Katherine Anne Porter*

I don't have a central metaphor for my life. I only have chaos. I now read that there is some kind of order even in chaos, and that's comforting.

—*Louise Erdrich*

I was not looking for my dreams to interpret my life, but rather for my life to interpret my dreams.

—*Susan Sontag*

Writing permits me to be more than I am. Writing permits me to experience life as any number of strange creations.

—*Alice Walker*

I've noticed that whenever I'm writing, I'm interested in everything, because I'm still waiting for the answer for the next page. I don't pay as much attention, when I'm not writing, to living in general.

—*Janet Lewis*

Writer's Life

As a writer you appear to be doing nothing most of the time.

—*Laurel Speer*

I expect that any day now, I will have said all I have to say;
I'll have used up all my characters, and then I'll be free to get on
with my real life.

—*Anne Tyler*

The most peculiar thing about it is that when you write you are
required to think and having once noticed that, you observe how
little the rest of life makes such a demand.

—*Elizabeth Hardwick*

No matter how we seek to disguise the unpleasant fact, a poet
remains a person whose life is essentially unjustified and justifiable:
her "calling" is simply to *be*, to experience, and to metabolize that
experience through the process we call poetry.

—*Jan Claussen*

The best thing you can have in life is to have someone tell you a
story.

—*Leslie Marmon Silko*

Aging

The old woman I shall become will be quite different from the woman I am now. Another I is beginning.

—*George Sand*

My mind is changing dramatically as I move toward fifty. And I imagine fifty as some sort of a gate; the door is going to open and I'm going to be somebody else.

—*Paula Gunn Allen*

Time and trouble will tame an advanced young woman, but an advanced old woman is uncontrollable by any earthly force.

—*Dorothy L. Sayers*

Little old ladies is the term they use to make us laugh at the women who have been fighting for sixty years.

—*Alta*

One thing is certain, and I have always known it — the joys of my life have nothing to do with age.

—*May Sarton*

Aging

What a wonderful life I've had! I only wish I'd realized it sooner.

—*Colette*

Springtime is a season we tend to forget as we grow older, and yet far back in our memories, like the landscape of a country visited long ago, it's always there.

—*Kay Boyle*

After a certain number of years, our faces become our biographies.

—*Cynthia Ozick*

The good thing about becoming older is that you gain time from that much more experience and can see where the real stories are.

—*Gail Godwin*

My work is less an obsession than it was when I was young because I've been able to write the major portion of what I have to say. It has always been a hard joy.

—*Jane Rule*

Aging

The mind of a post-menopausal woman is virtually uncharted territory.
—*Barbara G. Walker*

What I want to do is draw middle-aged women out of their purdah, make them really joyous. Menopause is the invisible experience. People don't want to hear about it. But this is the time when everything comes good for you - your humor, your style, your bad temper.
—*Germaine Greer*

It is perhaps only in old age, certainly past fifty, that women can stop being female impersonators, can grasp the opportunity to reverse their most cherished principles of "femininity."
—*Carolyn G. Heilbrun*

After a woman passes manopause she really comes into her time. I feel that. I've never felt so well or had so many images before me.
—*Meridel Le Sueur*

Aging

All one's life as a young woman one is on show, a focus of attention, people notice you. You set yourself up to be noticed and admired. And then, not expecting it, you become middle-aged and anonymous. No one notices you. You achieve a wonderful freedom. It is a positive thing. You can move about, unnoticed and invisible.

—*Doris Lessing*

Being an old maid is like death by drowning, a really delightful sensation after you cease to struggle.

—*Edna Ferber*

I doubt that I shall have affairs or bother my children when they are grown, for my real passion always goes to writing.

—*Michele Murray*

When men reach their sixties and retire, they go to pieces. Women go right on cooking.

—*Gail Sheehy*

As you grow older, you'll find that you enjoy talking to strangers far more than to your friends.

—*Joy Williams*

I was what's called, rather unhandsomely, "highly sexed." But it was such a surprise that one could attract. It was like a stream finding out that it could move a rock. The pleasure of one's effect on other people still exists in age — what's called making a hit. But the hit is much rarer and made of different stuff.

—*Enid Bagnold*

An archeologist is the best husband any woman can have; the older she gets, the more interested he is in her.

—*Agatha Christie*

Preparing for the worst is an activity I have taken up since I turned thirty-five and the worst actually began to happen.

—*Delia Ephron*

Aging

Neither for men nor for women do we anywhere find initiation ceremonies that confirm the status of being an elder.

—*Simone de Beauvoir*

I do not want to die until I have faithfully made the most of my talent and cultivated the seed that was placed in me until the last small twig has grown.

—*Kathe Kollwitz*

The lovely thing about being forty is that you can appreciate twenty-five-year-old men more.

—*Colleen McCullough*

People ought to be one of two things: young or dead.

—*Dorothy Parker*

People tend to think that life really does progress for everyone eventually, that people progress, but actually only *some* people progress. The rest of the people don't.

—*Alice Walker*